ALIVE
IN
CHRIST

A Devotional

HELEN TEO WALTON

PARTRIDGE

Library of Congress Control Number: 2019912593
ISBN: Softcover   978-1-5437-5358-5
                 eBook   .   978-1-5437-5359-2

Print information available on the last page.

To order additional copies of this book, contact
Toll Free 800 101 2657 (Singapore)
Toll Free 1 800 81 7340 (Malaysia)
orders.singapore@partridgepublishing.com

www.partridgepublishing.com/singapore

Acknowledgements

To our heavenly Father, who initiated the redemption plan; our Lord Jesus Christ, who came for us; and the Holy Spirit, who today guides, leads and empowers us in Christ.

A special thanks to the following for your prayers, support, feedback and encouragement:

> Jessica Ho, Bermie Dizon, Mervin Walton, Matthew Teo, Kathy Ross, Angela Wee, Celeste Ang, Maria Koh, Ewon Lee and Rod Sundholm for taking time to read the initial manuscript. Your valuable feedback in the early stage was instrumental in shaping the final outcome of the book.
>
> Thank you Lakshika Hettiarachchi and Tesa Mandias for your prayer support and encouragement.
>
> A very special thank you to Anna Teo for your prayers, encouraging words and faithfulness in reading the draft, editing, and the final proofreading. Thank you for your valuable and honest feedback and your labour of love.
>
> The followers of Alive In Christ https://www.facebook.com/aliveinchristscriptures/ for visiting the page all these years. You have shown me that in today's world, the internet is a valid place for people to share, partake of Jesus and His love and encourage one another in Him.
>
> My husband, Mervin Walton, for your prayer support and agreement with me for this book.

To all who read this book —may you grow from glory to glory in Christ Jesus.

Christ in us, the hope of glory (Colossians 1:27 NKJV)

This book is adapted from the Christ-centred, Spirit-led Facebook devotional page Alive in Christ, which has been encouraging and grounding believers in their identity in Christ since 2015: https://www.facebook.com/aliveinchristscriptures.

These devotionals point to God's love for us as manifested by His beloved Son, Jesus. They focus on Jesus—who He is, what He did for us, and what we inherited because of His finished work at the cross. They point readers to look to Jesus for every area of need or lack and to establish their hearts strongly and soundly on the love that Jesus has for us. In Christ alone lie our peace, joy, meaning, purpose, and solid foundation in this troubled world.

The work of the Holy Spirit is an integral part of our lives. We come to the fullness of all that God has for us through the leading of the Holy Spirit. By focussing on Jesus and meditating on His love, goodness, and finished work instead of dwelling on our circumstances, challenges, and health issues, we begin to hear more clearly the Holy Spirit's promptings and allow His power to work in our lives.

We believe that as you become grounded in God's love for you; in your identity in Christ, in all that Jesus has given you, and as you learn to be led by the Holy Spirit, your life will be transformed. Instead of fear, you will walk in hope. Instead of striving and being stressed, you will begin to thrive and be rested. Instead of being in bondage to destructive habits, you will be set free to pursue your hopes and dreams. You start to enter into the abundance that God has for you—the fullness of His love, peace, joy, favour, healing, blessings, protection, provision, and thriving in all you do.

This book is especially helpful for the pre-believer and new believer to be established in the basic truths of the Gospel. But it is also beneficial for any believer, as it will ground you more solidly in Christ.

We pray that this book will stir in you a desire to know more about Jesus and to grow in greater intimacy with Him. May you be transformed to enjoy all the beauty that God has for you. May you live in all the fullness of His love, peace, joy, provision and protection. May your path shine brighter and brighter in Christ Jesus, and may you live all the wonderful plans and dreams that God has for your life.

All scripture references are taken from the following versions.

CONTENTS

Day 1—God Knew You Even before You Were Born

> Before I formed you in the womb I knew you; Before you
> were born I sanctified you; I ordained you a prophet to the
> nations. (Jeremiah 1:5 NKJV)

You are not an accident. You are not an insignificant nobody. You are special to God. It is God Himself who formed you, created you, and put His mark on you. Even before you were born, He already sanctified you. He set you apart for Himself. You were meant to be in relationship with Him, to walk and talk with Him, to hear from Him, to dance with Him, and to live in the fullness of His love, joy, peace, and all the wonderful plans and dreams He has for you.

But how is that possible? For the longest time, you have felt inadequate, insignificant, and inferior to others. You have felt like you have achieved nothing and that you are a failure. You are beset by fears, anxieties, and a sense of hopelessness. You feel condemned because of failures and mistakes of the past. You feel so unworthy of anything good. Take heart, my friend. God has a life for you that is filled with peace, gladness, and joy. You can thrive at what you do, feeling fulfilled, satisfied, and connected to a divine eternal purpose.

The truth is that when God formed you in the womb, He already sanctified you, set you apart, and laid out a wonderful plan for your life. This plan was hijacked, and so many of God's children have ended in a place far below what God had intended for us. But God has already brought restoration so we can become reconnected with Him and dwell in the highest place He has for us.

It doesn't matter how you feel right now; you may feel unloved, insignificant, tired of trying, unhappy, and unsatisfied. It doesn't matter what you have done in your past or the pains and hurts that trouble you. The truth is that you are special to God. God does not define or esteem you the way the world does or the way your feelings tell you. He sees you as His beautiful, lovely creation regardless of what work you do, how much or how little education you have, where you live, and how much or how little money you have.

His greatest desire is to have a relationship with you. He wants to talk to you, to fellowship with you. Above all, He wants you to receive freely and enter fully the wondrous, glorious life that He has for you.

He knows with all our failings, mistakes, pride, and lowly thinking that it is not possible for us to enter into relationship with Him, and that is why He provided a way for us to come into relationship with Him and receive the fullness of His life through His Son, Jesus Christ.

As you follow the writings in this book, take time to ponder, open your heart to receive, and take it in because God has so much better for you.

You may pray with me.

> Dear heavenly Father, as I read this book, open my heart to Your ways and thoughts, especially to see that Your thoughts towards me are good. Help me to grasp the extent of Your love for me, to comprehend that You have wonderful plans and dreams for me, and to grasp that You have so much more that You want to pour into my life. Open my eyes to see, and open my heart to receive Your love. Amen.

Day 2—The Beginning of Man

> And the LORD God formed man of the dust of the ground, and breathed into his nostrils the breath of life; and man became a living being. (Genesis 2:7 NKJV)

> For **the life** of **the** flesh *is* **in the blood** (Leviticus 17:11a NJKV)

God thought about us from the beginning and wanted to give us life because He wanted to have a loving, delightful relationship with us. I imagine God must have thought of different ways to bring us into being from nothing. And decided that He would use the dust of the earth to create the first man, Adam.

Adam came to life when God breathed into him. At that first breath from God, imagine blood started flowing through that clump of dust that God formed, and life began for Adam. God's heart must have been bursting with love when Adam took his first breath.

When blood was formed, life began. God tells us from way before any scientific discovery that the life of the flesh is in the blood. He knows because He is the One that created life. Medical science caught up in the last century, discovering that red blood cells carry oxygen that is required for the heart and the brain to function. A lot more has been studied and written about blood and stem cells. But the Bible preceded science telling us that life is in the blood.

So Adam himself bore the breath of God. Man represented by Adam came from God and has the essence of God's breath. Man is delightfully created by one creative stroke of God. And life flowed through Him when blood was formed! In that way we are indelibly connected to God.

Take time to imagine and mull over how God created Adam, how He caused blood to flow within him and life started. How awesome is that! What a wonderful, creative God. And He is our heavenly Father who loves us and gives us life.

Day 3—God Created Man in His Own Image

> Then God said, "Let Us make man in Our image, according
> to Our likeness; let them have dominion over the fish of the
> sea, over the birds of the air, and over the cattle, over all the
> earth and over every creeping thing that creeps on the earth."
> (Genesis 1:26-27 NKJV)

Not only did Adam bear God's breath, but God also made him in His own
image. Adam was created like God in His essence of love, peace, joy, patience,
kindness, goodness and desire for relationship. Adam was supposed to live a
delightful life growing into the fullness of God's essence, and in relationship
with Him. Just as He is Father, Son, and Holy Spirit in relationship with one
another. Adam was to become the model for all mankind.

Not only that, God also gave Adam the dominion over all the earth. It meant
that Adam had power and authority over everything, every creature that lived.
Imagine he could command the lions and tigers and they would have to obey
him. He could decree and call forth the plants and trees to flourish and they
would obey him. Adam was supposed to influence man and nurture him to
look to God as his heavenly Father, in relationship with him, receiving counsel
and instructions on how to exercise his dominion on the earth. In doing so,
man would mature fully into all that God created him to be.

God did all of that because He longed to have human children, who, through
the dominion and authority given him would become fully mature in His
essence. He created Adam and gave him a wife, Eve, to enjoy everything that
He created. He loves us and His one desire is to grow in relationship with us,
walking and talking with us and gifting us with every good thing.

> Dear heavenly Father, give me a greater understanding of
> Your desire to have a relationship with me. Open my eyes
> and my heart to hear and receive from You that I may know
> You more. Amen.

Day 4—The First Sin Of Man

> And the LORD God commanded the man, saying, "Of every tree of the garden you may freely eat; but of the tree of the knowledge of good and evil you shall not eat, for in the day that you eat of it you shall surely die." (Genesis 2:16-17 NKJV)

> Then the serpent said to the woman, "You will not surely die. For God knows that in the day you eat of it your eyes will be opened, and you will be like God, knowing good and evil." (Genesis 3: 4:5)

God then showed Adam and Eve the tree of life and the tree of the knowledge of good and evil and gave them one command. They could eat from every tree, except from the tree of the knowledge of good and evil. If they did that, they would die (spiritual death).

The command not to eat from the tree of the knowledge of good and evil was to ensure that Adam and Eve believed and trusted God wholly. As Creator, God is the source of all that is good, lovely, beautiful, delightful and divine. Outside of Him would be the opposite. It was therefore important that man trusted God alone and only received from Him. His desire was for man to be pure, prefect and untainted to eventually enjoy all the glories and beauty of heaven.

The serpent in Genesis 3 represents the devil who is the enemy of God. The devil is jealous because God loved man and has good plans for him. The serpent would try anything to destroy man's relationship with God. He challenged Adam and Eve on the very thing that God told them not to do. He told them that God lied to them, and that by eating from the tree of the knowledge of good and evil, they would become like God. See the lie? Adam and Eve were already created in God's image; they were already like Him. The devil is the big liar.

Unfortunately, Adam and Eve succumbed to the devil's lies and distrusted God instead. They brought all mankind with them, on a path paved by the devil.

Day 5—All of Mankind Was Born with Adam's Sin Nature

> At that moment their eyes were opened, and they suddenly felt shame at their nakedness. (Genesis 3:7a NLT)

> "Cursed is the ground because of you; through painful toil you will eat food from it all the days of your life. (Genesis 3:17b NLT)

> And Adam lived one hundred and thirty years, and begot a son in his own likeness, after his image, and named him Seth. (Genesis 5:3 NKJV)

Sin is when we refuse God, reject Him, and choose to follow our own ways. By trusting the devil over God, Adam committed the first sin of man. When Adam did that, he allowed the devil to have dominion, have a say, over him. From the beautiful, lovely, joyous, thriving and peace-filled life that God had for him, Adam became cursed to live in sorrow, toil, and sweat, dominated by the devil.

Because the devil now had dominion over Adam, through Adam, he also gained the dominion over the earth that God gave to Adam. The devil was now in a position to wield his influence over the earth as well as over man.

The Bible further tells us in Genesis 5:3, 'Adam ... begot a son in his own likeness, after his image, and named him Seth.' After Adam's fall, all mankind—yes, you and I included—were born in his likeness, in his fallen way, separated from God, under the dominion of Satan, where sin, disobedience, pain, sorrow, and sickness thrive.

God's original plan was for man to walk in love, peace, joy, health, hope, patience, kindness, goodness; the essence of God. But sin; not trusting God, rejecting Him, brings severe consequences. When we do not trust God, and refuse His counsel, we are not receiving from Him. If we are not receiving from Him, then we are receiving from another source, the devil, who now has dominion and influence over the world. He has nothing good for you. He is jealous of you and only has lies to keep you away from God, who is the source of all that is good, lovely, beautiful, delightful, divine and eternal.

Now that the devil has dominion over the world, man has become subject to what the devil brings; pride, ego, greed, lies, cunning, hatred, impatience, shame, condemnation, sickness, stress, fears, anxieties, bondage to what destroys, depression, hopelessness; every bad thing you can think of. Do you now see clearly why the world has all these problems? Have you yourself been subject to some of these? We have all been lied to by the devil at some point in our lives and suffered the consequences but there is good news.

God was neither surprised nor shocked by what Adam did. He knew what the devil was like. God already had a secure, contingent plan to rescue man, and to establish him more securely to Himself. It is a plan in which the devil would be defeated for good, his dominance over man broken. It is a plan where man would be made perfect and holy so that He can continue in eternal relationship with God.

God's plan was to send His own Beloved Son, Jesus, who is God Himself, perfect, holy, completely obedient to God, and without sin. He would come in the form of man, yet is totally God. His divine blood would be shed for mankind.

At man's creation, God breathed into Adam, blood formed and man came to life. This time, the Son of God will shed His blood so that all who believe in Him will be born again to a new spiritual life. Christ's divine blood flows through him giving him eternal life, uniting him with God for eternity. And the devil can't do anything about that!

> Heavenly Father, open my eyes to all Your ways. Open my heart to see and grasp all that took place from Adam's time to Jesus's sacrifice. Speak to my heart, and change my heart so I can receive all Your truths. Amen.

Day 6—The First Animal To be Sacrificed for Sin

> At that moment their eyes were opened, and they suddenly
> felt shame at their nakedness. So they sewed fig leaves
> together to cover themselves. (Genesis 3:7 NLT)

> And the Lord God made clothing from animal skins for
> Adam and his wife. (Genesis 3:21 NLT)

When Adam and Eve disobeyed God, their eyes were opened, and they saw
that they were naked. They felt shame and tried to cover up their nakedness
with fig leaves. Instead, God used animal skin to cover their nakedness.

The fig leaves were Adam and Eve's own idea to cover up their shame. This
act represents man's own thinking, works and efforts to placate God. The
covering that God made for Adam and Eve was made of animal skin. An
animal (that did no wrong) was killed, and its blood was shed.

Sin is serious to God because it leads man away from Him. Not only from
Him, but also from the wonderful, joyous life He has for them in this world
and the glorious eternity with Him. Because life is in the blood, therefore
blood is required to restore life back from sin and death. This first sacrifice
of blood in Eden was a precursor for a greater sacrifice for the world.

Throughout the rest of the Old Testament, we see the continued sacrifice of
animals and the use of their blood to cover for sin. When God gave Moses the
system of sacrifices and offerings for the atonement of sin, He was preparing
fallen mankind, pointing them to the time when He would send His only
beloved Son as the perfect sacrifice to die the death that was ours because of
Adam's sin.

> Heavenly Father, help me to comprehend and trust You and
> the depth of Your love, grace, mercy, wisdom, and divine
> ways. Thank You for such a marvellous way to restore us to
> Yourself. Thank You that throughout the ages, You love me,
> and Your love for me never wavered. Amen.

Day 7—The Practice of Animal Sacrifice in the Old Testament

> For the life of the flesh is in the blood, and I have given it
> to you upon the altar to make atonement for your souls; for
> it is the blood that makes atonement for the soul. (Leviticus
> 17:11 NKJV)

In the Old Testament, God gave Moses a total of 613 ceremonial, moral and religious laws which had to be perfectly kept. Curses would befall anyone who failed to keep any law perfectly. God knew that it was not possible for anyone to fulfil these laws perfectly. So in His mercy to keep them from suffering the curses of breaking the law, God gave a system of sacrifices and offerings to the children of Israel as atonement when they broke any law.

These living sacrifices—an ox, calf, or pigeon—had to be perfect, free of blemishes and diseases. The sinner would lay his hand on the animal, taking on the animal's purity and perfection while his sins are transferred to the animal. The priest would then kill the animal and the animal's blood was offered at the tabernacle as atonement for sin. Because the life is in the blood, only the shedding of innocent blood can atone for sin, which leads to death, and bring back life.

God was and is seriously against sin. It took the blood of a pure, unblemished animal to atone for the guilt of sin and return a sinner to innocence and purity. Each sacrifice covered sin for a time — monthly or yearly — and then a new set of offerings had to be made for new sins committed. This sacrificial system given to Moses pointed to the Saviour of the world who would become the perfect Sacrifice, shedding perfect innocent blood, to save mankind from sin and death.

> Heavenly Father, You have provided a marvellous way for the
> forgiveness of my sins. Thank You that You have given me
> Jesus as the final, perfect sacrifice so that my sins are now
> forgiven me. Give me more revelation and understanding of
> Your love for me. Amen.

Day 8—The Precious Blood of Jesus

> Not with the blood of goats and calves, but with His own blood He entered the Most Holy Place once for all, having obtained eternal redemption. (Hebrews 9:12 NKJV)

> But with the precious blood of Christ, as of a lamb without blemish and without spot. (1 Peter 1:19 NKJV)

The sacrifices of animals under the Mosaic Law atoned for the sins of the children of Israel. They were really pointing to the perfect sacrifice for all mankind, Jesus Christ. Only the divine blood of Jesus, the Lamb of God, can cleanse the whole world's sins. No human is fit to make this sacrifice because all are born tainted with Adam's sin nature.

Jesus, God's own beloved Son, came to earth as a man. He was conceived by the Holy Spirit. Medical science tells us that an embryo is formed when a sperm meets an egg. At that point, blood develops, and life begins for the embryo. The male element meeting the egg results in blood being formed and life starting. The male element in the conception of Jesus is the Holy Spirit. Medical science also tells us that the mother's blood does not mix with the blood of the embryo throughout the whole pregnancy. Therefore Jesus's blood came from the Holy Spirit, the male element. His blood never interacted with His mother's blood, so although human, He was truly God, divine, perfect and spotless.

How wonderful is the love and infinite wisdom of God! When He created mankind and the reproductive process, He already had in mind the way to bring Christ, fully man yet fully God with divine blood, to redeem our sins.

Jesus's blood offered to our heavenly Father in the Most Holy Place in heaven is what cleanses the sins of the world. His blood shed for us reversed what Adam did. He brought us back into trusting God again. And He made us pure, holy and acceptable to our heavenly Father. He set us free from the Adamic nature and in return, we receive His life. Continue to read on and learn how Christ has made you a totally new creation, set free from Adam's sinful nature and the devil's dominion.

Day 9—God Did Not Send Jesus to Condemn the World

> For God did not send His Son into the world to condemn the world, but that the world through Him might be saved. (John 3:17 NKJV)

God did not stop loving mankind despite Adam's disobedience and distrust of Him. God's love is unconditional and eternal. He is kind, merciful and full of goodness towards us. He showed His wonderful love for us by sending His beloved Son, Jesus, into our life here on earth.

Jesus, Son of God, holy and divine, came as a man into the midst of the problems, illnesses, temptations, failures and brokenness of mankind. These are the consequences of Adam's fall. Jesus came and absorbed all the sins and failures of man upon Himself. He did this, shed His blood and died on the cross, in order to give to us a more wonderful and heavenly life.

God sent Jesus to take on this lowly and humiliating task of redeeming mankind because only someone with a divine nature could lift us into a relationship with God. No efforts, sacrifices, or works of fallen man can make us right and acceptable and bring us into a relationship with God the Father.

Above all, God wants a relationship with you because He loves you. He sent Jesus so that through His death and resurrection, the devil is now defeated; and his dominion over you destroyed. Jesus's blood shed for you has cleansed you of Adam's sin of disobedience to God and all other sins; they came from that one sin. He has restored you to walk in freedom from the power of the devil and of sin.

Jesus did not come to condemn you. He came to save you from an eternity under the devil's dominion. Your heavenly Father loves you, you are precious to Him. He wants you to come freely to Him to enjoy fellowship with Him and to receive His wisdom, counsel, favour, blessings and guidance. Through Jesus, you have been restored to walk in all the good plans that He has for you. What a wonderful salvation!

> Heavenly Father, thank You for loving me and for sending Jesus. Help me to comprehend and grasp Your love for me. Give me a greater revelation of Your wondrous love for me. Amen.

Day 10—God Loves You but Hates Sin

> But God demonstrates His own love toward us, in that while we were still sinners, Christ died for us. (Romans 5:8 NKJV)

Many of us grew up with the idea that God was out to get us, to punish us for our sins. Have you ever felt that way about God? That is far from the truth. God is not looking at your sins and failures, or your past. The truth is that He loves us but hates sin. He hates what sin does to us. Sin has consequences that destroy us. Sin wields its punishment on us. Sin brings about condemnation, and it causes us to move further from Him and not turn to Him for divine solutions.

In His love for us, God does not even have any requirement for us to use our own efforts or sacrifices to make ourselves acceptable, sinless, and pure to Him. This is an impossible requirement as long as we have the fallen Adamic nature. Instead, God sent His beloved Son on our behalf. Only He can reverse the Adamic nature and give us a new nature. Jesus came when we were in the midst of our sins, failures, and fallen nature, and He did everything necessary to redeem us from that fallen nature. His work is finished. God's only requirement is that we believe Him and follow Him

That is how much God loves you and me. He sent His beloved Son while we were still sinners, not after we tried to clean ourselves up. Rejoice today. Think no longer of past mistakes and sins, but be ever conscious of how much your heavenly Father loves you. Receive His love for you, be filled with His love and grace, and allow His love for you to transform you to overcome sin and the destructive consequences of sin.

> Dear heavenly Father, I so desire to be transformed into who You designed me to be: a beloved son/daughter walking in the fullness of Your love, forgiveness, peace and joy. Help me, Lord, to be open and to learn from You, to keep my mind and heart on You and Your love. Amen.

Day 11—We Are Made Right with God by Believing in Jesus

> Knowing that a man is not justified by the works of the law but by faith in Jesus Christ, even we have believed in Christ Jesus, that we might be justified by faith in Christ and not by the works of the law; for by the works of the law no flesh shall be justified. (Galatians 2:16 NKJV)

The children of Israel had to obey every law to walk in the blessings of God; otherwise, curses fell on them. In His mercy, God gave a system of offerings (in the form of an unblemished animal) to atone for their sins so they were spared the curses and could instead walk in God's blessings. As the sinner placed his hand on the spotless animal, his sin was transferred to the animal and the animal's innocence to him. God now saw the people as innocent as the sacrificed lamb (Leviticus 4:32–35).

The law did not make anyone right. It condemned the sinner. *The animal sacrifice was what made the sinner right with God.* Likewise, today we are made right not by our works, charity, sacrifices, offerings, or trying to keep a set of rules. God Himself gave us a pure and innocent offering in Christ Jesus, our perfect Lamb.

No amount of sacrifice, doing good, charitable works, or prayers can make us right with God. Simply believe and trust in Jesus as your sacrificial Lamb. Make Him the Lord and Saviour of your life, the Master of your soul. When you do that, our Father sees the purity and perfection of Jesus on you, making you right, perfect, and acceptable to Him.

> Lord Jesus, I ask that You help me to grasp all the wonderful truths that I am reading. Open my spiritual eyes to see and take in the wondrous things You have done for us. Open my heart to know You more and more. Amen.

Day 12—Jesus Came as God's Sacrificial Lamb for All Mankind

> Then Jesus came with them to a place called Gethsemane, and said to the disciples, 'Sit here while I go and pray over there.' And He took with Him Peter and the two sons of Zebedee, and He began to be sorrowful and deeply distressed. (Matthew 26:36–37 NKJV)

Have you ever felt unworthy of God's love? How can it be that He cares about you? As you see the extent of Jesus's suffering, know this: He did it with you in His heart and mind.

Jesus's intense suffering at the hands of mankind started at the Garden of Gethsemane. He knew the time had come for the completion of the redemption plan of His Father. The sacrificial Lamb was about to be offered for the sins of mankind. He was in such agony thinking of the suffering ahead that He sweated blood.

He prayed three times that the cup of suffering be removed. But three times, He submitted to His Father. The motivation for His submission: you and me. Whilst in agony, terrified at the prospect of what the people would do to Him, His heart was focussed on you and me. He knew that if He passed the cup of suffering, it would thwart His Father's redemption plan for all mankind, and we would continue mired in the sin nature with no help, lost for eternity.

This is how much Jesus loves you. You are precious to Him, and He willingly became subject to the fears, pain, suffering, torture, mocking, and humiliation for your sake. He was willing to be spat at, blasphemed, and die a slow, painful, humiliating death on the cross to redeem you and give you victory over all these things.

> Lord Jesus, thank You for Your sacrificial love for me. Thank You for all the suffering that You took on my behalf so that my sins are forgiven. Help me to understand and receive Your love that I be filled with it. Amen.

Day 13—Jesus Was Found Not Guilty, yet He Was Condemned

> When the chief priests and officers saw Him, they cried out, saying, 'Crucify Him, crucify Him.' Pilate said to them, 'You take Him and crucify Him, for I find no fault in Him.' (John 19:6 NKJV)

After His arrest, Jesus was pushed from Annas to Caiaphas, to Pilate, the Roman governor who sent Him to Herod, who upon finding no fault with Him sent Him back to Pilate to be charged. All this was done through the night and morning.

Pilate declared Jesus not guilty several times (Luke 23:22). In his reluctance to crucify Jesus, Pilate offered an alternative: set free Jesus, or set free a convicted rebel and murderer, Barabbas. The people chose to set free Barabbas.

The Old Testament offering of the innocent lamb to be slain was unfolding in reality. Jesus, pure and sinless and judged innocent, was sentenced to death on the cross. He was abandoned by His own disciples, even denied. He was tortured, beaten, spat at, humiliated, blasphemed, and struck by soldiers. He had a crown of thorns pierced into His head and was finally nailed to the cross for a slow and painful death. The sinner's hand was laid on the innocent Lamb.

To place our hands on Him is to believe He is the Son of God, the perfect Lamb of God. Our sins are transferred to Him and His righteousness to us. Start seeing yourself as set free from sin and guilt because of Jesus. What a way to honour our Lord and Saviour, by receiving His gift of righteousness.

> Thank You, Jesus, for Your sacrifice and love. Help me, Lord, to yield my thoughts and feelings at the cross and receive Your abounding love and life anew each day. I desire to receive Your abundant forgiveness and live free of guilt and condemnation. Amen.

Day 14—The Extent of Jesus's Love for Us

> And He, bearing His cross, went out to a place called *the Place* of a Skull, which is called in Hebrew, Golgotha, where they crucified Him. (John 19:17–18a NKJV)

Jesus died a humiliating death: crucifixion, hanging on a cross. Crucifixion was a most brutal form of punishment resulting in a slow and painful death. It was a degrading form of punishment reserved for slaves and extreme criminals of the day.

On the way to Calvary, Jesus was mocked, laughed at, spat upon, scourged, beaten, tortured blindfolded, blasphemed, and struck by soldiers. A crown of thorns pierced into His head, He was finally nailed to the cross for a slow and painful death. Jesus was perfect, He was without sin, He had none of the evil corruption that is in the fallen human heart—yet He took all that darkness onto Himself, all the way from Gethsemane to the cross. He paid a heavy price to set you and me free.

Jesus was the divine redemption to which the sacrifices of the Old Testament were pointing. The pure and sinless Lamb of God was finally offered for all mankind's sins. He took upon Himself our sins. He paid a heavy price for our redemption. In return, He gave us His righteousness, His holiness, His perfection, and His purity.

By Jesus's sacrifice, God wants you to know that you are totally forgiven and accepted. You are now adopted sons and daughters of the Most High God. Through Jesus, you have become totally pure and holy in the Father's eyes.

> Thank You, Jesus, for Your sacrifice and Your grace. Help me, Lord, to grow in greater revelation and understanding of Your love for me and that I have been made righteous by your sacrifice. Help me to keep my heart open to You, Your love and truth. Amen.

Day 15—Jesus Provided The Way To Our Heavenly Father

> And Jesus cried out again with a loud voice, and yielded up His spirit then, behold, the veil of the temple was torn in two from top to bottom; and the earth quaked, and the rocks were split. (Matthew 27:51 NKJV)

> Brethren, having boldness to enter the Holiest by the blood of Jesus, by a new and living way which He consecrated for us, through the veil, that is, His flesh, and *having* a High Priest over the house of God, let us draw near with a true heart in full assurance of faith. (Hebrews 10:19-21a NKJV)

In the Old Testament, the Holy of Holies was the most sacred place in the Tabernacle. It was the place where God dwelt. A thick veil separated the people from this holiest place of God's presence because, in the fallen state, the brightness of God's glory would have been too much to behold.

When Jesus died at the cross, Matthew 27:51 tells us that this temple veil was torn in two from top to bottom. Jesus's sacrifice removed the veil that separated us from coming directly into God's presence.

Hebrews 10:20 tells us that Jesus's own flesh has replaced the veil and His flesh now provides us a new and living way to come face to face with our heavenly Father.

By His one sacrifice at the cross, Jesus cleansed you of all your sins. When you trusted Jesus to be your Lord and Master, you were made righteous, pure and holy in your spirit. You can now come freely into God's holy presence!

> Thank You Lord Jesus for Your sacrifice, for Your flesh that made a way for me to come freely before my Heavenly Father. Thank You for Your great love for me. Teach me and show me how to walk fully in the salvation that you have given to me. Amen.

Day 16—Come in Repentance to Jesus Who Took Your Sin

> The next day John saw Jesus coming toward him, and said, 'Behold. The Lamb of God who takes away the sin of the world.' (John 1:29 NKJV)

Have you ever felt such shame, guilt and condemnation because of what you have done? And you tried to make yourself feel better by doing charitable works or being good and generous to others? You felt better for a while but soon the guilt and condemnation came creeping back. Have you been there?

Whatever we try to do to remove our shame and guilt is like Adam and Eve using fig leaves to cover their nakedness. That will not do. Our heavenly Father Himself has made garments for us, by the death of an innocent, pure and holy Lamb. The shedding of His divine blood produces the garments of righteousness that has the power to remove sin, shame, guilt and condemnation.

Jesus, the holy Lamb of God, was sacrificed at the cross for you. His blood washed away your sins completely. There is no sin too big, or too shocking, for which Jesus's finished work cannot atone. You may have done the vilest thing and you think God despises you. No. God loves you. He sent Jesus to be the sacrificial Lamb so that you can be set free from the power of sin, guilt and condemnation.

Your heavenly Father desires more than anything to see you turn in repentance from your old ways of sin and come to Christ. It delights Him when you walk in the victory over sin that He has given to you through Jesus. He longs for your fellowship and to walk with you and guide you along the good path that He has for you, in the fullness of His love, peace, and joy. Will you come to Him?

> Dear Jesus, Thank You for dying on the cross for me and for being my Saviour and Master. I desire to grow in greater understanding of You and Your love for me. Teach me and help me to grow in You. Amen.

Day 17—Jesus Supplies the Water That Brings Everlasting Life

> But those who drink the water I give will never be thirsty again. It becomes a fresh, bubbling spring within them, giving them eternal life. (John 4:14 NLT)

Being made in God's image, we have a thirst in us, a craving, an unquenchable longing for the divine. To quench this thirst, however, man resort to all kinds of pursuits. What is your pursuit? Is it a career? Is it material wealth? Is it to look fabulous and flawless? Is it to have the admiration of others?

The pursuit of fame leaves many insecure, unsatisfied, lonely, and troubled. The pursuit of wealth often does the same, without the rewards of lasting happiness or relationships. The pursuit of power and position leaves one with no peace or joy, isolated and unable to trust. The pursuit of happiness is elusive.

This scripture tells us that those who drink the water that Jesus gives will not thirst again. The water of everlasting life is His Spirit living within us. His Spirit of wisdom, knowledge, comfort, love, peace, joy, and ability to overcome all things. He is the Spirit that brings us the Father's love, and reminds us of all that Jesus has done to set us free from the power of sin. He shows us our Father's heart towards us. He leads us to receive what He has given to bless, protect, favour, heal and restore us so that we can walk in the good and pleasant paths that our Father has ordained for us.

Have you been disappointed, disillusioned or disenchanted? Come to Jesus. He will not disappoint. He wants to fill your heart with His Spirit and give you His life, peace, joy, love, satisfaction and a divine sense of purpose.

> Holy Spirit, I invite You to move freely in my life and draw me close to You. I give You permission to do the work of removing all my fears, doubts, and anxieties. Let Your fountain of love, peace, and joy spring up within me. Teach me to be more and more yielding to Your ways. Amen.

Day 18—Jesus Is the Bread of Life That Satisfies

> I am the bread of life. He who comes to Me shall never hunger, he who believes in Me shall never thirst. (John 6:35 NKJV)

> And the LORD God formed man of the dust of the ground, and breathed into his nostrils the breath of life; and man became a living being. (Genesis 2:7 NKJV)

Adam came to life when God breathed into him. At that first breath from God, blood started flowing and life began for Adam (life is in the blood). Not only does man bear God's breath, but he was also made in God's own image. He was created to be filled with God's love, joy, peace, and character and to live a delightful life in relationship with Him.

God gave us life and we are indelibly connected to Him no matter how far off we are from Him. It is no surprise that within each person is a deep longing for a relationship with the God who gives us breath and life. Jesus, the beloved Son of God, is the only one who can satisfy that deep longing, emptiness, and hunger within you for the divine. He is the bread that satisfies and fulfils so that you may never hunger or thirst again. When you come to Him, His Spirit comes and lives in you, filling you with His shalom peace and satisfaction.

How do I come to Him? You can call on Him, praise Him, thank Him, glorify Him, and talk with Him. In His presence you will find peace and joy. Bask in it. Spend time to read His Word, meditate on it and ask Him to illumine your mind as you read. Let your heart and mind be filled with the knowledge of His abundance of forgiveness, love, joy, peace, patience, goodness, favour, healing, and every good thing.

Be still and receive His love and hear in your heart what He is speaking to you. He wants you to know how much He loves you. He knows every detail of your life and He delights in you. You are His precious child.

Day 19—Put Your Confidence in the Lord

> It is better to trust in the LORD than to put confidence in
> man. (Psalm 118:8 NJKV)

People have put their trust and confidence in man and man-made solutions, and they have been disappointed time and again. They compromise their values in the pursuit of love, fame, wealth, validation, acceptance and security. Do you relate to this? Or does it describe someone you know?

All the pursuits of man stem from what lies in the heart: a need and desire to be loved, validated, and accepted, and to feel secure and free of fear. But no man, no system, and no institution can satisfy these needs. Neither can any amount of wealth or fame fulfil these longings. Only God alone can meet and satisfy the deep desires of the heart for love, acceptance and validation.

People are not always faithful, and neither are they always merciful and unconditional in their love. They are also not always dependable. Even if they are, they grow tired and weak, lacking the resources to meet our needs. But our God has every resource and ability to meet our needs, and His love towards us is even greater.

God is always faithful, good, merciful, and forgiving. His love for you is unconditional and unwavering. He is totally trustworthy and dependable. His heart is all for you, and His thoughts are always of good towards you. He is able and willing to meet all of your needs. He loves you so much that He gave you His most beloved Son so that you can come into the heavenly abundance that He has for you. Come to Him and trust Him. He will not disappoint.

> Father God, I thank You for Your love for me, for Your
> faithfulness, and for Your mercy and grace. Help me to let
> go of areas where I have put my trust, whether it is in another
> person, a boss, a career, an organisation, a ministry, or the
> economy. Help me, Lord, to trust You completely in all these
> areas, and to rest in You. Amen.

Salvation Prayer

Our heavenly Father desires more than anything for you and me to come into fellowship with Him and be restored to the divine nature that only Jesus can give us.

If you are unsure whether you have this relationship with your Creator, or you would like to enter into this relationship with Him, fellowship with Him, enjoy His companionship, and receive freely the wonderful, glorious life that He has for you, then you can pray this simple prayer. As you pray, mean it with your heart, yield your life to Him, and invite His Spirit and peace to come dwell in you.

> Dear heavenly Father, I thank You that You love me. I desire to come home to You. I thank You for Jesus, Your Son whom You sent so that I can come freely to You. Dear Jesus, I thank You for dying on the cross for me. I invite You to be the Lord and Master of my life. Help me and teach me so that I can grow in greater knowledge and understanding of Your love and grace. And help me to yield to Your truth, love, and Spirit. Thank You, heavenly Father. Thank You, Jesus. Amen.

Day 20—Jesus: The Perfect Sacrificial Lamb

> For as by one man's disobedience many were made sinners,
> so also by one Man's obedience many will be made righteous.
> (Romans 5:19 NKJV)

Do you come from a religious background where sacrifices, charity, good works, and church attendance were practiced in such a way it seemed that was the way to earn salvation, favour, and acceptance with God? And when you fell short, you fell into condemnation and thought God must be upset with you? This makes the Christian life heavy and burdensome, and that is far from God's truth.

Jesus died for us, forgave us, and made us acceptable to our heavenly Father. Just as by Adam's fall, man became fallen, so by Jesus's obedience, man is made righteous. We are accepted by God not because of our good works or character but because we have chosen to believe Jesus and follow Him. In Christ alone are our perfection, holiness, and acceptance.

If you struggle with condemnation, always thinking you're not good enough or have not done enough, here is good news: it is the finished work of Jesus that makes you acceptable to God, not what you have done or not done. In Christ, you are already forgiven, favoured, loved, accepted, blessed, healed, protected, and supplied with all that you need.

No more wondering if you've done enough or if you've unknowingly missed anything and incurred God's displeasure. He is not looking at you; He is looking at Christ in you. It is not about you. It is all about Christ, the perfect sacrificial Lamb, and His obedience and finished work. You are loved and favoured because you believe Jesus.

> Dear Jesus, help me to grasp this truth that I have been forgiven and made righteous by Your sacrifice. Renew my mind to this truth. Thank You for Your sacrifice for me. Amen.

Day 21—He Conquered Sin for Us

> And having been perfected, He became the author of eternal
> salvation to all who obey Him. (Hebrews 5:9 NKJV)

Jesus was completely without sin, totally obedient and in perfect relationship with His Father. He died for our sin, setting us free from its power and in return, making us righteous. When you invited Jesus to become the Lord of your life, you opened your heart to Him. You chose to follow Him rather than the world's thoughts (dominated by the devil) and by your own self-focussed and limited ways.

Are you struggling with your weaknesses and failures—or worse, steeped in pride and judgement towards others? Stop and look to Jesus and see how beautiful, lovely, and perfect He is. Start to see yourself in His image. No matter what sins—you could be living a homosexual lifestyle, or maybe you are addicted to drugs, alcohol, and other destructive habits, or you have anger issues, or you have a critical attitude towards others—Jesus has the power and ability to turn your life around if you let Him.

Keep coming humbly to Jesus with your desires to turn from your old ways. His love, His help is there to lift you to overcome your weaknesses. He alone has the power and ability to restore you to right living.

When you first came to Him, you already received His forgiveness. So start to see yourself righteous and holy in God's eyes. Do not let the thoughts and temptations fool you to think that you are still a sinner. In Christ, you are a saint made perfect from the inside. In the face of temptations, keep looking to Jesus, who is your salvation. When you do that, you allow His Spirit to supernaturally transform you from within.

Take time to thank Jesus for giving you eternal salvation. Ask Him to help you to see yourself as righteous and beloved because of His finished work. Spend time to dwell in His presence and take in His love for you.

Day 22—He Did Not Die Just for Christians; Everyone Qualifies

> And He Himself is the propitiation for our sins, and not for ours only but also for the whole world. (1 John 2:2 NKJV)

Jesus died to give us God's life. He died for the whole world, for everyone, no matter what religious background you belong to. It doesn't matter that you may be into witchcraft, you are rich or poor, educated or not, incarcerated, or hopelessly lost in drugs or alcohol.

His death and sacrifice is for you, meant to bring you into God's life and kingdom, which is forgiveness of all your sins. You can be set free from guilt and condemnation, enjoying His eternal love, joy, and peace. His work for you is already finished. It's for you to receive Him, believe Him, and appropriate all that He has done for you.

Our sins and the consequences of our sins may make us feel disqualified to receive His love and grace. The truth is anyone who has ever sinned qualifies. Don't let your mistakes, failures, what you think of yourself, or your religious background disqualify you.

God loves you, and by Jesus's death on the cross, He qualifies you to receive the abundant life that He so wants you to enjoy. Simply believe and look to Him. When you believe Him and invite Him to be your Lord and Saviour, your old life of sin died with Him at the cross. In His resurrection, you were raised to new life in Him. His Spirit now dwells in you. God loves you so much and has made it so easy for you to be saved.

> Dear Jesus, I thank You for dying on the cross for me. I acknowledge that there is nothing I can do to make myself right and acceptable to God, except to receive the sacrifice of Your love. I invite You to become the Lord and Master of my life. I yield every area of my life to You—my thoughts, my emotions and all my ways. Thank You for being my Saviour. Amen.

Day 23—You Are so Deeply Loved

> May [you]… comprehend … the width and length and depth and height—to know the love of Christ which passes knowledge; that you may be filled with all the fullness of God. (Ephesians 3:18–19 NKJV)

God is love, and when He created us, we necessarily bear His essence—love. Therefore we are created with love defining our core being; we are created to love and to be loved. When we are loved, we become who God created us to be: valued, special, secure, precious, and capable individuals. When we are loved, we esteem ourselves better, and we have a grounded-ness and security to step out, love in return, thrive, and be all that God created us to be.

Unfortunately, the world has departed far from the love of God. Maybe you grew up being told you were not good enough, not smart enough, not beautiful enough. You got compared with others and fell short. You were not given the affirmation that you are worth loving.

God wants you to know that you are so dearly loved by Him. You are special to Him. He wants you to live to the full potential of who He created you to be. That's why He emphasises the many dimensional aspects of His love—if only you knew the width, length, depth, and height of the love that Jesus has for you.

You are the apple of God's eye. His love is a healing balm, healing you from deep within of hurts, pains, wounds, and abuses. He's restoring you to walk in the fullness that He has for you. See Him there in your pains, hurts, neglect and abuses. See His love reaching for you. Take time to dwell on how deeply loved you are, how special you are to Him. Receive His love, enjoy and bask in it, enter into His peace and joy. Begin a wonderful journey to walk with Him and in the abundance of His love for you.

> Thank You Jesus for Your love for me. Help me receive Your love anew each and every day. Amen.

Day 24—May You Know His Great Love for You

> Now may the Lord direct your hearts into the love of God
> and into the patience of Christ. (2 Thessalonians 3:5)

The love of God is unlike any love that the world knows. His love is kind and unselfish unlike human love which is often self-serving. His love is forgiving, unconditional and sacrificial, unlike the world's love which often hinges on our good behavior or actions. His love is about giving the best to us.

He is always patient no matter how we have failed or messed up. His heart grieves when we allow the cares of the world to wear us out. When we are steeped in bondages to habits and substances that destroy, He patiently waits for us to come round to Him. No matter how deep and dark a place you are at, He never stops loving you. He never gives up on you. His love for you remains strong. He loves you so dearly with His love that is pure, perfect and unchangeable. It expects nothing from you yet has every good thing to give to you.

He showed His love by giving us His Beloved Son Jesus who left heaven's beauty, to take on man's limited and lowly flesh. His ultimate purpose was to suffer and die a slow, humiliating, painful death at the cross so that you and I can escape an eternity separated from His love and life. He willingly sent His most beloved Son to suffer and die for you.

God's greatest desire is to direct your heart to His love. He wants you to know the strength and the extent of His love for you. More than anything, He wants you to receive His abounding love. Because in receiving and functioning in His love is where you find your true worth - valued, special, secure and precious. Will you open your heart to His love? Just come to Him, quieten your thoughts, sit with Him and let Him saturate you with His beauty, kindness, goodness and peace. Keep on coming to Him to receive His love and be filled.

> Lord Jesus, thank You for loving me and giving Your life
> for me. Open the eyes of my understanding and give me
> revelation knowledge of Your love for me. Amen.

Day 25—He Defeated Sin, Death, and the Devil

> Having disarmed principalities and powers, He made
> a public spectacle of them, triumphing over them in it.
> (Colossians 2:15 NKJV)

Sin, death and the devil go hand in hand. Sin is rejecting God, refusing His life, and His provisions for us. The devil is all out to deceive man into sin, to keep us separated from God. He keeps man living in bondage, fear, anxiety, depression, sickness, defeat, hopelessness, and condemnation; blinded to God's love, fatherhood and help. He puffs man up in pride and self-glory, into thinking that he does not need God. The ultimate end of living out of relationship with God is eternal death.

Praise Jesus that at the cross, He defeated the devil and the power of sin and death. He disarmed the devil when He gave us eternal life, setting us free from death. He disabled the power of sin to condemn and destroy us when He forgave us and washed us free of our sins. His Spirit now dwells in us. Sin, death and the devil has lost all power to defeat us. He has also given us a heavenly life of love, peace, joy, favor, protection, healing and blessings. Lack, fear, anxiety, defeat, depression, condemnation is no longer our portion in life.

Therefore, instead of focussing on your mistakes, weaknesses, problems, and challenges and becoming overwhelmed with more fears and anxieties, come to Jesus, rest in Him for He has defeated the devil and all his works. He has triumphed over all those negative forces that try to come against you. He won this victory for you. In Him, you have been set free to walk in relationship with Him; in faith, peace, joy, gladness of heart, victorious and thriving in life. Let your heart rest on the victory that you have in Christ. Put on an attitude of confident dependence on Him and speak in agreement with His truth.

> Thank You, Lord Jesus, for defeating sin, fear and death
> and giving me the victory over them. Help me to draw close
> to You. Fill me fully with Your love, peace and joy. Amen.

Day 26—We Can't Save Ourselves

> …but now, once at the end of the ages, He has appeared to put away sin by the sacrifice of Himself. (Hebrews 9:26a NKJV)

When you first invited Jesus to be Your Saviour, you were forgiven and received His righteousness, love, peace, joy and hope. But you find yourself still steeped in bondage to alcohol, sexual problems, anxieties, fears, and have no peace. You feel powerless and condemned. Where is the power to overcome your problems? How is it that you are still like before; you lose your temper, you are still weak, you get fearful and anxious, unable to resist the same temptations.

There is nothing you can do to remove sin or the effects of sin—the despair, condemnation, and hopelessness. It is not about church going or trying your best to overcome your problem. Jesus, His love for you and His sacrifice at the cross is the power for you to overcome sin and its consequences!

His one sacrifice at the cross and His blood has washed you free of your sins and declared you free of condemnation. When He died at the cross, your old sin nature, the old you, died with Him. When He rose from the dead, you rose with Him to a new victorious life. Know this truth. Keep it in your heart, on your lips - you have been made righteous by His blood. He loves you greatly. In Him lies the power to overcome your weaknesses.

Come to Jesus and see His perfect love for you. He wants you set free from sin, condemnation, fears, and anxieties. He wants to see you living victoriously, in His peace and joy. Hold on to the truth, and declare often, that in Him, you are no longer a sinner. You are righteous, you are no longer powerless and without help. You now have His victory, peace, joy, favor, blessings. Keep on coming to Him to receive His love and grace that will lift you and empower you to walk righteously, in wholeness and fullness of life.

Day 27—In Christ, You Died to Your Old Life

> I have died with Christ who now lives in me. And I now live
> by faith in the Son of God, who loved me and gave his life
> for me. (Galatians 2:20 CEV)

When Adam chose to disobey God, he led all mankind to be born with his nature—the sin nature. Jesus went to the cross to reverse what Adam did. At the cross, Jesus received the punishment that Adam's sin deserved. By taking that punishment for us, He set us free. There's no more punishment for us but life everlasting instead.

When we invite Jesus to be our Lord and Master, we repudiate and renounce that sinful nature that we inherited from Adam. Our old selves – the sinful, rebellious, defiant nature– died along with Christ's death. When Jesus rose again, you rose with Him, and this time your nature is replaced by His divine, glorious, righteous nature. You no longer have the sin nature of Adam. God has made it so easy for us to enter into eternal life with Him.

Be confident that Christ truly dwells in you. Do not look at your behaviour and reason that it is not possible. You may at times still lose your temper and fall into sin, but the truth is that Jesus lives in you. He has given His life for you.

Be patient with yourself and ask for His help. Whenever you fall, come to Him and receive His love. When you are sincerely sorry for what you have done, He is ready to pick you up and strengthen you to walk more gloriously.

> Thank You, Jesus, for dying for me. Thank You that because
> of You, all my sins are forgiven. Thank You that I can indeed
> walk in freedom from all my past sins. Teach me how to
> walk closely with You, and help me to know You more and
> more. Thank You Lord. Amen.

Day 28—Your Sins Are Not Counted against You

Blessed is the man to whom the LORD shall not impute sin.
(Romans 4:8 NKJV)

King David knew the joy of being freely forgiven. Living under the Law of Moses, David should have been stoned for adultery. Yet he was not and went on to become the family line under which Jesus was born. King David was not just reflecting on his own situation—he was looking at us today.

He was looking to when Jesus would come and bear our sins and in return give us His righteousness and holiness. How blessed we are to live in this time where we are completely forgiven because of Jesus's finished work at the cross two thousand years ago. It's not by our own works, sacrifice, or good behaviour; there's nothing to do with us. It's everything to do with Jesus's sacrifice at the cross. What a glorious way to be forgiven and live righteous with God, simply believing and inviting Jesus to be the Lord and Master of your life.

We heard a testimony about prisoners, toughened by years of rough living and crime. When they heard about how much God loves them, how much He cares about them, that He sent His son Jesus to die for them to forgive their sins, these men broke down in tears. They were so touched that seven hundred of them surrendered their lives to Jesus. The prison authorities saw real change in the men months after this event. They saw peace and joy that was not there before. These men were truly set free. How blessed to live knowing all our misdeeds and crimes are forgiven, and we are loved.

When you receive His forgiveness, you also enter into a satisfying and fulfilling relationship with Him. He has given you a glorious eternity with Him but He also has good plans for you and a blessed life and future here on earth. The Lord is bidding you to come to Him, talk with Him, hear Him, bask in His presence, and receive fully every hope and dream He has for you. Take some time now and thank Him for everything.

Day 29—In Christ, You Overcome the World

> Who is he who overcomes the world, but he who believes
> that Jesus is the Son of God? (1 John 5:5 NKJV)

When Jesus became your Saviour and Master, the Holy Spirit came to live
in you. The Holy Spirit is the very life of God—love, joy, peace, patience,
goodness, favour, healing, self-control, and wisdom. All the power and
supernatural help you need to overcome the problems and challenges of life
is now in you.

Are you discouraged because of a bad habit? Perhaps it's a drinking problem,
or a problem with drugs, gambling, or pornography? You say, 'I can't kick
this problem. I feel helpless and weak. I've had this problem for so many
years.' Whatever situation you are facing, you can overcome it with Jesus. You
already have His Spirit, His ability in you to overcome all things.

We know brothers who were addicted to drinking and smoking, but as
they kept looking to Jesus and declaring with their mouth that Jesus had
made them righteous, declaring that the Holy Spirit now lived in them, they
supernaturally lost the desire to drink or smoke.

Stop looking to yourself; stop beating yourself up for failing. Stay rested and
keep your eyes on Jesus and His love, compassion, perfection, and faithfulness.
Declare that you are made righteous because of Him. Make Him the centre of
your life. As you yield to Him, you are allowing the power of the Holy Spirit
to work in you. He alone can supernaturally set you free from any bondage
or addiction.

> Thank You, Lord, for loving me. Thank You for Your blood
> that has made me righteous. Thank You for the Holy Spirit
> who now dwells in me, empowering me to overcome addictive
> habits and behaviours. Lord, I surrender my struggles to You
> and ask that You take over. Overwhelm my thoughts with
> Your thoughts, love, and ability. Amen.

Day 30—Salvation and Blessing Are from the Lord

> Salvation *belongs* to the Lord. Your blessing *is* upon Your people. (Psalms 3:8 NKJV)

Have you ever tried hard to get out of fears, anxieties, loneliness, and depression? No one is able to save himself from these, or from diseases, addictions, and habits that destroy. We may turn to medication, therapy, and counselling. Man have tried all ways and means, introducing different ways of thinking, philosophies, systems of belief, and new medication to try to save the world around him. But at best, these help people to cope with their problems without treating the root cause or providing a permanent cure.

Jesus alone gives lasting, eternal salvation and forgiveness. He delivers us, protects us, and brings lasting and enduring healing. He brings joy, peace, and restoration. He alone has the power to set us free from destructive habits, uncontrollable anger, anxieties, and depression. He is the source of life, and being connected with Him is where we find complete salvation—that place of rest, truth, clarity, completeness, joy, and divine purpose.

He keeps our path straight. His peace that surpasses understanding keeps us sound and grounded. His love and protection sets us on a solid, unshakeable foundation in spite of turmoil around us. His Spirit in us empowers us to overcome sin, to reign over destructive habits, to thrive in challenging situations. He beckons you to come to Him with open arms and receive from Him. Come into His presence and receive His love. Let Him take your anxieties and cares. And receive His peace and love in return. Let Him flood you with His goodness and joy. He is always there waiting for you.

> Thank You, Jesus, that You are my Lord, Saviour, and Master. I receive Your peace, joy, and healing. Draw me close to You, and help me as I keep my focus away from what does not edify. Help me to keep looking to You and to bask in Your love and freedom. Amen.

Day 31—You Are Sealed with the Holy Spirit

> In Him you also trusted, after you heard the word of truth,
> the gospel of your salvation; in whom also, having believed,
> you were sealed with the Holy Spirit of promise. (Ephesians
> 1:13 NKJV)

When you put your trust in Jesus, you were sealed with the Holy Spirit, who now lives in you. You have been marked and sealed by God. You belong to Him. You now have the life of God, the life of Christ in you. His Spirit of power, love and of a sound mind, wisdom, counsel, understanding, might, comfort, peace, joy and ability to overcome all things, now resides in you. You now have the ability to process situations like Jesus does, with His compassion, wisdom, and intelligence.

You say, "How can it be? I still feel the same way and don't sense that anything has changed." Well, immediately after you say your marriage vows, you won't suddenly feel like a different person from the day before, but the reality is you are now married and have a significant other in your life. In spite of not feeling any different, it does well for you to spend time with your spouse, communicate with, get to know him or her better, and build a wonderful marriage.

When you invited Jesus to be your Lord and Master, the Holy Spirit came and dwelt in you. You may not feel any different. But He now lives within you. He is God's seal on you that you now belong to Him. He is gently nudging you to come into His presence. He delights for you to spend time with Him. He beckons you to read His Word and be aligned with His thoughts towards you. Take time, quieten yourself and hear your spirit resonates with His truth and be refreshed by His love, peace and joy.

> Holy Spirit, I thank You that You now dwell in me. Open
> my eyes and my heart to see more and more of Your love,
> guidance and leading in my life. Help me to be yielded to
> You. Amen.

Day 32—Father, Son, and Holy Spirit Dwell in You

> If anyone loves Me, he will keep My word; and My Father
> will love him, and We will come to him And make our home
> in him. (John 14:23b NKJV)

There is a condition before God makes His home in you: that you love Him
and keep His word. In the New Covenant context, to love God is to love Jesus.
To keep His word is to believe that Jesus is truly God's own Son; He is the
way, the truth, and the life. He is the way that God has ordained for us to be
reconciled with Him. In Him is also the power to overcome sin.

How awesome that God the Father, Son, and Holy Spirit has now made His
home in you. You are truly the dwelling place of God, His tabernacle, the place
where He dwells. The enemy cannot do anything to harm or destroy you.

You have God's life in you. That means you have all His power and ability
to remain always victorious, regardless of the circumstances or symptoms.
No fear, anxiety, curses, sickness, and disease can overwhelm you or squash
you without your permission. No trial or problem can overtake you and
overwhelm you. You can overcome all things because the One through whom
all things are possible dwells in you.

His life in you also yields wonderful fruits of love, peace, joy, humility,
kindness, goodness, patience to enable you to walk righteously. The more
deeply you walk with Him, the more of these fruits will manifest in you.
Come to Him often. He longs for your companionship. He is your loving
Father who longs to lavish you with His love, joy and goodness.

> Lord Jesus, thank You for first loving me. I love You, Lord.
> Thank You, for giving me Your life and making Your home
> in me. Help me to be sensitive to Your presence within me.
> Help me as I long to walk closely with You and bear fruits
> that glorify You. Amen.

Day 33—God Wants Us to Have His Nature

> And because of his glory and excellence, he has given us great and precious promises ... that enable you to share his divine nature and escape the world's corruption caused by human desires. (2 Peter 1:4 NLT)

There is a search in the natural man's heart for the spiritual. This is because we originated from God. We received life when God breathed His breath into us. It's no wonder that many in the world are spiritually sensitive. Unfortunately, they also have no knowledge of God's ways, no knowledge of His love, His grace, of Adam and of Christ. They end up exploring the spiritual through witchcraft, sorcery, fortune telling, geomancy, psychic readings, etc. These are the playground of the devil to trap man in eternal spiritual darkness.

As a child of God, you no longer have to resort to these spiritual outlets. You belong to God, and He has much better for you. In Christ, you have received God's life. The Holy Spirit lives in you and you have access to His help, His leadings and His gifts. He has wonderful spiritual gifts waiting for you to bless you as well as for you to bless others. He wants to fill you with holy desires and fulfil your heart's longing for the divine and for eternity.

If witchcraft, psychic readings, or involvement with ungodly spiritual practices have been a part of your life, realise that God is greater, far more superior than any other spirit. God longs for you to come and receive from Him and be set free from bondage to evil. He loves you and does not condemn you. He longs to fellowship with you and bless you with every good thing. Come to Him now. He has a wonderful new life for you.

> Heavenly Father, I repent of my ways. Thank You that You have forgiven me through Jesus, my Lord. Open my spiritual eyes, lead me, and help me to be sensitive to Your leading and guidance. Give me the wisdom and strength to yield to You, submitting to You in all my thoughts and ways. Amen.

Day 34—He Can Save Completely

> Therefore He is also able to save to the uttermost those who come to God through Him, since He always lives to make intercession for them. (Hebrews 7:25 NKJV)

Jesus continues His ministry today, interceding for us to freely receive the fullness of our Father's love and provision in all areas of our lives. He desires more than anything to restore each person to our heavenly Father.

Do you have loved ones who are living a lifestyle of sin, lost, depressed, rebellious, chronically sick, and addicted to drinking and other substances? Take heart and continue to pray for them that their hearts are softened and they turn to Jesus. Because He can save and restore completely what has been stolen from them – the years, relationships, joy, success, a thriving life.

Years ago, a family member was diagnosed as bipolar. For the longest time, she manipulated the family and gave endless heartache and pain. It was challenging dealing with someone who was irrational and manipulative. When I understood the redeeming power of Christ and started to pray for her, she opened up and shared a secret she'd borne the guilt of for over thirty years. I shared with her how Jesus has already forgiven her at the cross. She invited Jesus to be her Lord and Saviour. Today, she is well and restored, gets along with people, and lives her life in relative peace and joy. Praise Jesus, who alone can save and restore even the most difficult persons and situations.

Regardless of how hopeless you think your problem is, Jesus is able to completely save. He can restore peace, joy, relationships, and even time. In the face of eternity, time—the minutes, hours, days, weeks, months, and years—is not of the essence. More than anything, He wants your heart, and He is patient enough to wait. He wants for you to be able to come freely to fellowship with Him and walk in the fullness of all that our heavenly Father has for you.

Day 35—God Is Not Upset with You

> And you, who once were alienated and enemies in your mind
> by wicked works, yet now He has reconciled in the body of
> His flesh through death, to present you holy, and blameless,
> and above reproach in His sight. (Colossians 1:21–22 NKJV)

At one time, we were separated from God with our wrong thinking that He was mad and upset with us and that we were His enemies because of our sins. Today, there are still many who do not come to Him because they live in sin and think that God is angry with them.

The truth is God loves us and sent Jesus so that we can be set free, given a holy nature, and made clean to enter into a wonderful relationship with Him. When you invited Jesus to be your Lord and Saviour, He took great delight to present you holy, blameless, and without fault in God's sight. That is now your reality in Christ.

God wants all mankind to know that He has given a way out of sin and condemnation. It is not about church going; it is not about arguing whose theology is right and whose is wrong. It's not about following a set of rules of dos and don'ts. It is about knowing and being in fellowship with God, receiving the wonderful sacrifice that Jesus undertook for us at the cross, and being given a completely new nature, sinless and holy.

It is about having a relationship with Jesus; a greater intimacy with Him, being in worship and fellowship with Him, surrendering your thoughts and feelings to enjoy Him, being in His presence, basking in His joy and peace.

God loves you dearly and wants you to be in Christ, because that is where we walk in our true identity—holy, blameless, deeply loved, accepted, and connected to the divine, able to receive His wisdom, guidance and leading. Therefore keep looking to Jesus, come to Him in all things, spend time in His presence, receive His forgiveness, love and peace.

Day 36—In Christ, Your Sins Have Been Washed White as Snow

> Though your sins are like scarlet, they shall be as white as snow; though they are red like crimson, they shall be as wool. (Isaiah 1:18b NKJV)

God gave the children of Israel a system of offerings and sacrifices for the atonement of sins because He loved them and did not want them to suffer the curses that came with breaking the law. But the children of Israel came to a point where their hearts turned cold to God, and they were defiant towards Him. They continued their sinful, wayward ways and outwardly practiced the offerings and sacrifices to cleanse themselves. This grieved God greatly (Isaiah 1:14).

The story of the children of Israel serves to show the waywardness of the fallen nature. It was not possible for mankind in the fallen nature to have a meaningful relationship with God. Have you tried to overcome sin and bad habits using your own strength, only to fail and feel even more ashamed and further alienated from God?

Isaiah was prophesying of a time when God Himself would provide a failproof salvation for mankind so that, unlike the children of Israel in their rebellious ways, mankind would be set free from futile struggling in their own strength and effort to become right with God.

How blessed are we to live in this time that Isaiah prophesied about. It's not about how good you are, or what you have done. You are completely cleansed and forgiven because of Jesus. You are cleansed, declared righteous to be in relationship with God and the wonderful new life and plans that He has for you because of Jesus's sacrifice.

> Help me, Lord Jesus, to keep seeing myself totally forgiven because of Your blood shed for me. Cleanse my heart and mind of any guilt, shame, and condemnation. Or pride in my own abilities. Help me come to You daily and see Your love and beauty. Transform me with Your peace and joy. Amen.

Day 37—Sin Leads to Death; the Law Strengthens Sin

> The sting of death is sin, and the strength of sin is the law.
> But thanks be to God, who gives us the victory through our
> Lord Jesus Christ. (1 Corinthians 15:56–57 NKJV)

Death entered the world in the Garden of Eden when Adam sinned. Sin has affected every nationality throughout history—old and young, rich and poor, educated and uneducated. Sin has consequences: sorrows, pains, regrets, lost hope, lost innocence, guilt, shame, and condemnation. Sin is the poisonous sting that leads to death.

The law is what strengthens sin. The more we are told to not do something, the more we are challenged to do it. It's the response of the corrupt sin nature. The law simply shows up man's weaknesses and nature to sin. Through the law, people become aware that they have transgressed. The law pronounces them guilty and condemns them, and condemnation keeps them hiding from God.

Today, as a believer, you are no longer held under condemnation by the Law of Moses. Jesus, by becoming victorious over sin and death, has given us His victory over them. In Christ, we are not governed or condemned by a set of laws. The Holy Spirit dwells in us to lead, guide, and empower us to the most excellent standards of God so we can exceed beyond the requirements of the Law of Moses.

Start to see yourself totally cleansed and righteous. Renew your thinking with the Word and be yielding to God's truth. As the Holy Spirit transforms you, sin will lose its appeal to you. Whenever a thought comes to you that you know will lead you down a slippery slope of sin, turn your eyes back to Jesus and see His perfection. Day by day, become renewed and strengthened in your spirit and soul.

> Thank You, Jesus, that I can stand victorious in Your love,
> joy, peace, healing, blessing, provision, and favour, which You
> have freely given me. Help me to walk in Your victory. Amen.

Day 38—In Christ, You Are No Longer Dominated by Sin

> For sin shall not have dominion over you, for you are not under law but under grace. (Romans 6:14 NKJV)

Because of Jesus's sacrifice, God's love and His Spirit now dominates and moves you. You are no longer dominated by the devil or by sin. Neither are you governed by a set of laws that convict, punish and condemn you for failing. You have God's Spirit in you lifting you to the higher standards of God. When you submit to His promptings, His power will lift you to live more gloriously for Christ.

When you sin, falling for any of the devil's lies, you feel uncomfortable and uneasy. That is the Holy Spirit nudging you through your conscience, reminding you to live up to the new person that you are in Christ. When you submit to His promptings and repent (change your mind about what you have done), His power will lift you to live more righteously for Christ.

Therefore do not let sin lead you into condemnation, guilt and shame. God does not condemn you. God always hopes for you to keep coming to Him, no matter how you have sinned, so that He can restore you and lift you to His higher standards. The enemy on the other hand, will heap condemnation, shame and guilt upon you when you sin. These are his tools to rob you of peace and joy and keep you away from God.

God desires that you come to Jesus, repent, be cleansed and receive His love and strength to walk more righteously. He longs to see you set free from the power of sin and walk fully in the good plans that He has for you. Start seeing yourself righteous and holy in Christ. Yield to the Spirit's promptings and be set free from the power of sin.

> Thank You, Lord Jesus, for Your perfect sacrifice that set me free from sin. Thank You for the gift of the Holy Spirit, who leads me to walk in the power of Your love. Help me to be yielded to Your Spirit so that I can walk in Your victory. Amen.

Day 39—God Made Us Alive in Christ

> But God, who is rich in mercy, because of His great love with
> which He loved us, even when we were dead in trespasses,
> made us alive together with Christ (by grace you have been
> saved). (Ephesians 2:4–5a NKJV)

Did you ever have the idea that God is far away in heaven, easily angered when you sinned? I remember the early days of trying hard to win His forgiveness. The list of things I thought I needed to do was endless. It was tiring, and I never felt I was good enough.

Today's scripture tells us that God is rich in mercy and full of love for us. As a good parent who loves your child, you continue loving him even when he is willful and disobedient. You do not wish him bad. You continue to desire a good relationship with him, and to see him thrive and do well in his life. The love that you have for your child is merely a shadow of the love that God has for you. He is the source of love and you love only because He first loved you and put His love in you. His love is superior to any earthly parent's love.

Be rest assured that God is not upset with us because of sin. He loves us, but He hates sin. He hates what sin does to us – it robs us of the wonderful, delightful life that He has for us. He does not and never did count our sin against us but was waiting for a time to destroy its power in our lives.

Therefore have confidence. God loves you and when you come to Christ, you receive His power to overcome sin. God no longer sees you in your sins; He sees Christ in you. He sees you alive and full of His glory. Rest assured that sin is not your identity anymore. You have His divine life and ability to overcome the condemning power of sin and live victoriously for Him.

> Lord Jesus, thank You for loving me. I receive Your love and
> forgiveness. Give me more revelation of Your wonderful
> finished work so that I can walk more and more in Your love,
> peace, joy, contentment, and blessings. Amen.

Day 40—The Lord Corrects
Those Whom He Loves

> For the LORD corrects those he loves, just as a father corrects
> a child in whom he delights. (Proverbs 3:12 NLT)

If our sins are forgiven, does it mean we can go on and continue to sin? Absolutely not. God loves us and does not want us to persist in sin. Sin ultimately hurts us and those we love, keeping us from living in the satisfaction and fulfilment of the destiny that God has for us.

How does God correct us? He does not do so by giving us accidents and calamities. Or bringing diseases on us to teach us a lesson. He corrects us by His Spirit speaking to our conscience. The more we know God's Word, the more sensitive our conscience is when ungodly thoughts come to us or when we fall into sin. Our conscience helps us stay clear of and not entertain ungodly thoughts. When we fall into sin, our spirit becomes uneasy and disturbed. Have you experienced that? That's the Holy Spirit stirring your conscience, nudging you to come to Christ. He has given you the way to be restored to peace. Come to Him and receive His love, His forgiveness, and His help to change.

When a person numbs his conscience and persists in sin, God may correct him by letting him face the consequences of his sins. This could be disappointments, unnecessary sorrows, or regrets over lost opportunities. Instead of living in the glory of God's love, peace, and joy; sin, deceitful thinking, and rationalising cause us to end up unhappy and unfulfilled. And sabotaging the wonderful paths that God has for our lives. Praise God that it is never too late to come in repentance to Christ. He loves you and is ready to restore you. Hallelujah!

Therefore be humble, teachable, and yielding, because God corrects those He loves—not to punish but to bring us back to walk with Him on the path of righteousness in His love, peace, joy, glorious satisfaction, and fulfilment. He is a good heavenly Father who desires to see us walk in all the divine abundance He has for us because He loves us and desires to lead us on the path that leads to life.

Day 41—You Have Been Delivered from Darkness

> He has delivered us from the power of darkness and conveyed us into the kingdom of the Son of His love, in whom we have redemption through His blood, the forgiveness of sins. (Colossians 1:13–14 NKJV)

Not only were our sins forgiven when Jesus became our Lord and Master, but we became citizens of His kingdom. We are no longer citizens of this world, under the power of darkness. We are no longer tied to the sin nature of Adam but are set free to be citizens of heaven.

The powers of darkness, sin, condemnation, anger, addictions, all kinds of destructive habits, depression, and hopelessness no longer have hold over you. Are you still powerlessly addicted to drugs, powerless against the condemnation, hopelessness, and depression that this addiction brings on? The blood of Jesus has set you free.

Look to Jesus and see His love instead of condemning yourself for your wrong choices, failures, mistakes, and inability to control bad habits and behaviours. You are forgiven, and God does not condemn you. He loves you, and as you focus on Jesus, see His love and grace towards you, and yield to Him, His love will lift you.

Remember that you are no longer alone in your struggles. You are now a child of God, you belong to His kingdom, and you have His power and resources to overcome and be victorious over sin, set free from destructive habits so you can walk in peace and joy, in newness of life. Come to Jesus, quieten your heart and mind, sit with Him, talk with Him, enjoy His presence and receive His love.

> Lord Jesus, thank You that You have set me free from sin and all bondages to things that destroy. I am righteous because of You. I receive Your love, forgiveness and healing touch. Strengthen me, and guide me to walk in all Your ways. Amen.

Day 42—You Are Spirit, Soul, and Body

>...and may your whole spirit, soul, and body be preserved blameless at the coming of our Lord Jesus Christ. (1 Thessalonians 5:23b)

How are we holy when we still sin? Rightly dividing spirit, soul and body will clarify this. God is spirit and created us as spirit beings in relationship with Him. He gave us souls (our thoughts and emotions) and bodies, marked by the five senses and cravings. So we are spirit beings, with souls (thinking and feelings) and live in bodies.

When we invite Jesus into our life, our spirit is sanctified, made holy (set apart for God). His Spirit now dwells there. *Our recreated spirit* is the real person, the new creation in Christ, in eternal relationship with God. A person without Christ is still in the old sin nature, without eternity with God.

Our soul is not sanctified when we become believers. It is still conformed to the world and needs to be renewed by the Word of God (Romans 12:2). This part of us rationalises, reasons, and is filled with defeated or prideful thinking. It is also our emotions like fear, sadness, anger, happiness, joy, etc. Like the soul, *the body* is not sanctified when we become believers. Our body, governed by senses and cravings, is what needs to be disciplined (1 Corinthians 9:27); those ungodly cravings and desires put to death (Colossians 3:5).

Our unsanctified soul and body (also known as our flesh) will fall and sin as long as we are in this world. But God still calls us holy because He now looks at our recreated spirit where He sees Christ. He does not judge us by the sins and failures of our flesh. But He also does not want us dominated by our flesh and suffering the resulting consequences. He desires that we live by the Spirit, in His Word, strengthened in our inner man so that we can control the flesh.

When we renew and align our minds and thoughts to Christ's truth and love, it builds us to live righteously. Let's desire to be sanctified; spirit, soul and body, transformed to reflect His love and light to the world and then to dwell with Him for eternity! Amen.

Day 43—In Christ, You Are Now a Saint

> God from the beginning chose you for salvation through sanctification by the Spirit and belief in the truth. (2 Thessalonians 2:13b NKJV)

Many Christians grapple with this: 'How can I be a saint when I still sin?' When you invited Jesus to be your Lord and Master, an exchange took place in your inner being. Your inner spirit man, the real you, becomes totally recreated in Christ's identity. Your old sin nature was crucified on His body at the cross and when He resurrected, you resurrected with Him to new life, bearing His nature, His perfection and righteousness in your inner spirit man.

He became sin for you to set you free from your old self and give you a new life in Him! You are a whole new person in the spirit. But the outer man has not been transformed yet and needs to catch up with the inward spirit man. It needs to be renewed by the Word of God.

When God looks at us, He is looking at our inner spirit man. When we were born again, our inner spirit man changed citizenship. We are no longer citizens of the world but become citizens of heaven. We're no longer sinners but saints. Even though our outer shell still fails and falls into sins, it does not change who we are in our spirits.

If you have been seeing yourself a sinner, feeling condemned and ashamed, know that God wants you to start seeing yourself as you are in your inner man. Say this with me: 'I am a saint, beloved and accepted by our loving heavenly Father.'

> Lord, thank You that You have made me a saint. I so desire to live in the abundance of Your love, peace, and joy. I surrender my heart, my mind, and my life to You. Saturate me with Your love and presence. Grant my desire to freely enter into the wonderful journey of Your glorious grace and abundance. Amen.

Day 44—Believe, and You Will See

> But that no one is justified by the law in the sight of God is evident, for the just shall live by faith. (Galatians 3:11 NKJV)

You are made right with God and accepted by Him not because of the good works you do but because you believe in God, the Father; His Son, Jesus; and the Holy Spirit. God is not moved by your trying to do good to impress Him. Neither is He moved by your church attendance, fasting, praying, or Bible reading to win His approval, acceptance, and blessing.

One thing moves Him and touches Him: that you believe Jesus is His beloved Son who died on the cross so all your sins are forgiven. When you believe Jesus and what He did for you at the cross, it delights our Father. God has made it so simple for us.

As you walk closely with Jesus and experience His love, blessing, and fullness, you cannot help but be transformed. This is the life and experience of a true believer. As you grow in greater intimacy with Him, out of you flows His love, joy, peace, strength, and ability to overcome challenges. That's when people begin to notice a change in you, and they say things like, 'Hey you have changed. You're not the same person anymore.' Have you had people say that to you?

As you live by faith by believing Jesus, walking closely with Him, and trusting Him in all areas of your life, you enter more and more into the peace and joy that He has for you. You'd want to know Him more, draw into closer intimacy with Him, to fellowship, grow and share life with other believers, to pray, study, serve, and share His love. Walking by faith has transformed you, and you do all these not to be loved and accepted but out of the abundance of being loved and accepted!

> Dear Lord, I so desire to walk in closer relationship with You. Help me to always look to You. Amen.

Day 45—Trust in the Name of the Lord

> Some trust in wagons and some in horses. But we will trust
> in the name of the LORD our God. (Psalm 20:7 NLV)

As believers, it is easy to forget that God loves us, is able and can do all things for us. We become fearful and anxious about life. We forget that Christ is our supply and we resort to our own cleverness, to other ways and means to get on in life. We forget that He is our true foundation and we look for help and security in people, career, money, and sometimes, the government. How easy to go back to our old ways. Does this speak about you?

God does not stop loving you even when you forget to come to Him. He will never leave you nor forsake you because you are in Christ. Through Jesus, He has also made available the resources of heaven to you. He loves you and patiently waits for you to come to the end of yourself and trust Him. He is right there when you turn to Him and trust Him for all areas of your life. He is more than able and willing to help you. When you trust Him, He provides and His provision comes with satisfaction, peace and joy.

He wants to remind you that nothing in this world conjured by man is able to give you the satisfaction, fulfilment and security which you long for. Businesses can fail, wealth is lost, bosses fail you, careers end, the economy is shaken, and governments are weakened. But Jesus will never fail you. He is totally faithful and trustworthy. In Him you stand on a solid foundation. You remain in His shalom peace even when the unpredictable and unexpected happens. Therefore continue to put your whole trust in Jesus and not on any created thing or being. Trust in Him, and His Spirit will lead you in peace through the changing circumstances of life.

> Lord Jesus, thank You for Your love for me. Thank You that
> Your help is always available to me. I am sorry for the times
> that I fail to come to You. Give me a greater revelation of
> Your faithfulness. Help me Lord to draw close to You and
> to depend on You for all areas of my life. Amen.

Day 46—In Christ, No More Condemnation

> So now there is no condemnation for those who belong to
> Christ Jesus. (Romans 8:1 NLT)

Though we are forgiven and are now a new creation in Christ, what we have
done in the past may come back and start accusing and condemning us. Have
you found yourself in this situation?

Do not listen to those accusations. Jesus became our sin, died as our sin,
and in return gave us His righteousness, making us totally accepted by our
heavenly Father. You have been completely forgiven. It doesn't matter what
you have done in the past, what you have not done, where you have been,
or how bad you think you are. When you come to Jesus in repentance and
receive life from Him, your heavenly Father no longer sees you in your old
nature. He sees Christ in you.

God is not looking at your past, neither is He catching you at your failures.
He only desires that you don't fall into condemnation, and get so steep in guilt
and become too ashamed to turn to Him to receive His love. He doesn't want
you consumed by condemnation and thrown off the wonderful righteous path
that He has for you.

Your Heavenly Father's heart is that when you fail, and are truly sorry, that
you come freely to Him and receive His love, forgiveness and comfort. He
longs to fill the contrite and humble heart with His joy and peace and strength
to live gloriously.

> Thank You, Jesus, that You are the Lord and Master of my
> life. When I fail, help me to not fall into condemnation.
> Open the eyes of my understanding to start seeing myself as
> God sees me: I am the righteousness of God in Christ—pure,
> holy, totally accepted, loved, lovely, wonderful, gracious,
> kind, and beautiful. Amen.

Day 47—Jesus Makes You Righteous and Does Not Condemn You

> Who shall bring a charge against God's elect? It is God who justifies. Who is he who condemns? It is Christ who died, and furthermore is also risen, who is even at the right hand of God, who also makes intercession for us. (Romans 8:33–34 KJV)

Many little voices accuse us throughout the day. Voices tell us that we have failed as parents, as spouses, as siblings, as friends, as decent human beings. That we are not good enough, not smart enough, not good-looking enough, not successful enough, that we're just mediocre or that we'll never make it. Or some incident suddenly surface from the past and you become overwhelmed with guilt and shame. You start wondering, 'What if I had done this or that? If only I had …' All those thoughts and the regrets that you entertain can become arrows of condemnations jabbing at you.

Let it go. God loves you, and He doesn't condemn you. Today, Jesus continues to intercede for you. More than anything, He desires that you don't fall for the devil's lies. So don't give the devil any space and instead let your mind be filled with the words and thoughts of God, because He has good thoughts towards you.

He did not send Jesus to judge and condemn you. The devil is the one who is against you, the one who condemns you, the one who accuses you and makes you feel ashamed about your mistakes and failures. Satan makes you think that God condemns you so that you are too ashamed to come to Him.

Align your heart and words to agree with God's truth. Start to declare that you are beloved and accepted. Join Jesus as He intercedes for you. Decree and declare that you have been made righteous, that nothing the devil does can come against you and you will walk in His abundance and blessings. Declare that your path will shine brighter and brighter and you will walk from glory to glory in Christ Jesus.

Day 48—The Lord Redeems, Not Condemns

> The LORD redeems the soul of His servants, and none of those who trust in Him shall be condemned. (Psalm 34:22 NKJV)

God doesn't want you harbouring any condemnation that you have towards yourself. Condemnation usually stems from thinking God is angry and upset with us, and that can lead to sickness, fears, lost hope, and depression.

We had a neighbour who for years was under heavy medication for depression. After we got to know him, he shared how he used to be a top executive and lived a worldly life. Years later, he fell sick, and doctors couldn't diagnose his problem. Eventually he lost his job and his wealth. He started going to church but was told that God gave him the sickness as punishment for his sinful, worldly lifestyle. The more he heard this, the deeper he fell into depression. We shared the Gospel with him and how Jesus loved him and went to the cross for him. We assured him that God was not punishing him and that in Christ, he had been forgiven; God had a wonderful plan for his life. He continued to receive these truths through regular Bible study.

Within a couple of weeks, his countenance changed. He started smiling and would get up in the morning. He continued growing strong in the Lord and reduced his medication by more than half. He became active in a job that a friend had given him. He was set free from condemnation and walked in the freedom of peace, joy, and well-being in Christ.

The truth is God loves you, delights in you, and has given you His very best: His own beloved Son, Jesus. This truth about God's love for you will set you free from oppression, condemnation, and depression. Receive Jesus's forgiveness. Let His love cleanse you and restore you to walk in the freedom of His peace, love, joy, and the good plans He has for your life. Tell yourself each day how much Jesus loves you.

Day 49—You Have Been Set Free from Curses

> Christ has redeemed us from the curse of the law, having become a curse for us (for it is written, 'Cursed *is* everyone who hangs on a tree'). (Galatians 3:13 NKJV)

Under the Mosaic Law, one must perfectly fulfil every one of the 613 laws to enjoy God's blessings. Otherwise, curses, sicknesses, diseases, barrenness, and lack fell on the sinner (Deuteronomy 28). Praise God that Christ Jesus has set us free from this curse of the law.

Only Jesus could perfectly fulfil all the requirements of the law because He is spotless and sinless. His blood contains divine life, the only blood that can restore God's life to us. When He went to the cross, He became a curse (Deuteronomy 21:23). He did that for you and me, taking our place of being cursed and putting us in a place of blessing instead.

Rest assured that in Christ, no matter what you or your family has done in the past, all curses have been broken. It doesn't matter how many generations in your family has had a disease; when you are in Christ, the curse of that disease is not on you anymore. Generational curses ended when you come into Jesus. He bore these curses so you can be set free to enjoy the blessings of God.

Have full confidence to continue walking in close fellowship with Jesus and live out the good plans He has for you. Do not let your past—or the past of your parents, grandparents, or great-grandparents—affect you in any way. In Him, you have been set free from all curses. You are now a new creation, a beloved child of God. You have His life, full of possibilities and potential to live splendidly and excellently for His praise and glory.

> Thank You, Lord Jesus, that You have given me a completely new life, set free from generations of lack, poverty, sickness, pains, sorrows, addictions, and bad mistakes. You have set me free to live fully the wonderful, blessed life that is ahead of me. Help me, Lord, to grasp this truth and walk each day renewed in this truth. Amen.

Day 50—You Are Adopted as Sons of the Most High God

> Having predestined us to adoption as sons by Jesus Christ
> to Himself, according to the good pleasure of His will.
> (Ephesians 1:5 NKJV)

Do you sometimes wonder why others enjoy so much blessing while you seem to lag behind? Do you sometimes get envious of others' gifting, position in life, ministry, education, family, looks, and relationships? This can easily happen when we look at what others have and lose sight of all that God has given us. Envy keeps us wallowing in self-pity, and this prevents us from fully receiving every good thing that God has for us.

God wants to remind you that in Christ, you are now adopted into His family. You are now a child of the Most High God, with rights and privileges that only His children can enjoy. When you renew your mind to who you are and all you have in Christ, it will set you free to fully become the glorious person that God created you to be.

As His child, you are entitled to eternity with God; you are entitled to an intimate and close relationship with Him, to receive guidance and help from Him. You are entitled to His blessings, gifts, favour, and provision. In Jesus's name, you have His authority to decree and call forth what has been promised you, and to bind the works of the enemy. All things are possible with Him and as His child therefore, all things are also possible for you.

Keep seeing yourself as a son with rights, privileges, and benefits in the heavenly realm. What you have well surpasses what others have, and there is no need to look at and be envious of others. You already have all the heavenly inheritance because of Jesus.

Take time and thank your heavenly Father for adopting you into His kingdom through the wonderful, finished work of Jesus.

Day 51—In Christ You Are a Son of God

> For you are all sons of God through faith in Christ Jesus.
> (Galatians 3:26 NKJV)

When you believe Jesus as your Lord and Master, you are adopted into God's family. As a son or daughter, you are now a beloved family member with free access to what is in the heavenly kingdom.

Are you suffering from depression or feeling hopeless? You are a child of the Most High God, and His love, peace, and joy is yours. Are you suffering sickness and anxious to the bone? You are a beloved child, and His healing and restoration is yours. Are you feeling weighted down by burdens too heavy to bear? You are a beloved child, and He is ready and willing to lift the burden off you.

Don't disqualify yourself. Don't let your failures, mistakes, the past, and what you did or failed to do keep you from entering freely into your heavenly family and partaking of all that your heavenly Father has for you.

Everything that is in the kingdom of Heaven is yours to enjoy as a child of God. An intimate relationship with God, love, peace, joy, favour, healing, protection, restoration, success in relationships, and every blessing is yours. Your loving Father desires to see you at peace, satisfied, and enjoying all His wonderful blessings.

Therefore keep seeing yourself in your true identity. In Christ, you are indeed a beloved child of the Most High God, entitled to heavenly resources.

> Heavenly Father, thank You for loving me and adopting me into Your family. Thank You that I am now Your beloved child. Thank You for Your kindness and goodness towards me. I love You and desire to know You more, and to walk closely with you. Draw me close to You and give me fresh revelations of Your love and goodness. Amen.

Day 52—You Are Seated in Heavenly Places with Christ

> And raised us up together, and made us sit together in the heavenly places in Christ Jesus. (Ephesians 2:6 NKJV)

You may at times still feel anxious, fearful, and lousy about yourself. As believers, we all go through this. But the fact remains that in Christ, you are already seated with Him in heavenly realm. God wants to remind you that because you put your trust in Jesus, you have been raised from death and have new life with Christ in heaven. This is the truth, the divine reality, and it has nothing to do with your feelings.

It doesn't matter how you feel, or what is happening in your life or the world around you. Things may seem to be falling apart, but the truth is God loves you and has placed you in Christ, in a position unshakeable and solid, because He who saves you is completely faithful, dependable, and unchangeable.

You don't see the sun on a cloudy day, and everything seems gloomy, but the fact is that the sun is still there, shining. It's the clouds that are in the way. The fact remains that God loves you, and you have a place in His heavenly kingdom; it's your lousy feelings that keep you from seeing this truth.

Be patient and keep trusting in the Lord. He is much bigger than that problem, than that trouble, than those ugly rumours, than your fears and anxieties. Keep on seeing Jesus, and these will soon grow dimmer while God's love, grace, and peace become manifest.

Remind yourself, especially when you feel low, 'I am beloved and precious to my heavenly Father. I am the apple of His eye, and He will not withhold any good thing from me. I have been raised with Jesus and am seated with Him in heavenly places. I am filled with His love, peace, joy, and ability.'

Day 53—We Have a Good Shepherd

> I am the good shepherd. The good shepherd gives His life
> for the sheep. (John 10:11 NKJV)

A shepherd cares for and tends to his sheep. He protects them and leads them to safe and good grazing ground. His rod is used to ward off predators like wolves, and to check for dangerous under-growths. The shepherd's staff is curved at the end to recover a fallen sheep by hooking around the neck and pulling the animal to safety. The rod and the staff are never used to hit a sheep. Instead, it is used to protect the sheep, keep it safe, and lead it to good pastures.

Our Lord Jesus is our good shepherd. We are His precious sheep that He cares deeply about. He protects and keeps us from 'wolves' and other 'predators' that are out to steal our peace and joy and destroy us. He uses His rod to gently lead and guide us away from situations that could bring heartaches and hardships. Can you recall a time when you sensed a warning in your spirit not to enter a deal, a situation, and the people involved turned out to be crooks?

He is a good shepherd who wants the best for His sheep. Above all, He suffered and died for us in order to bring us under his shepherding so that He can lead us to every good thing our Father has for us. Because He is your shepherd, you will not lack or want in any area. You need not worry or be anxious because He leads us to good places, to green pastures, to quiet flowing waters where we can graze in safety, peace and contentment. You are protected. You are fully supplied with every pleasant thing that you need. His love, joy, peace, favour, surrounds you. You are in sound hands because He is a good shepherd who can be trusted totally.

He invites you to come to Him. You don't have to struggle by your own strength, isolated and afraid. Yield to Him and let Him lead you to a path of His love, peace, joy, protection, favour and thriving in all that you do. Take time and meditate on His love for you and how He shepherds you.

Day 54—In Christ, We Find Pasture

> I am the door. If anyone enters by Me, he will be saved, and will go in and out and find pasture. (John 10:9 NKJV)

Pasture is everything that is necessary for a deeply satisfying life abounding in peace, joy, and acceptance, where opportunities and doors open for us to thrive in our relationships, work, business, and everything that we set our hands and heart to do.

I remember the time when I was not in fellowship with God and was struggling in life. I was unhappy in my relationships and with my business, and my family problems seemed insurmountable. I was spiralling into depression because life seemed so bleak and hopeless. But when I came back to Christ, stopped depending on myself and yielded every area of my life to Him, things started to turn around.

He opened doors for me. Things at home settled down. As I trusted Him, believing in Him for all areas of my life, my life was transformed over the years. Today, my life overflows with the abundance of His blessing, peace, joy and satisfaction. Friends who knew me from twenty years ago comment how I have changed for the better, all by God's grace.

Do not be discouraged if right now you are not walking fully in the abundant life that God has for you. You may be beset with challenges, worries, and anxieties. Jesus says He is the door, and whoever comes through Him will be saved and find green pasture. God has a better, satisfying life with good pasture that He has made available to you through our Lord Jesus.

Keep looking to Jesus, read the Word to know His thoughts. Come to Him, and spend time in His presence. In all things, look first to Him, trusting Him and drawing peace, joy and hope from Him. It will start happening. Suddenly, you'll find things getting better and better. Suddenly, unexpected good doors open, and a new life thriving in peace, joy, favour, hope, and satisfaction begins to unfold. Amen.

Day 55—He Is Light, and in Him There's No More Darkness

> I have come as a light into the world, that whoever believes
> in Me should not abide in darkness. (John 12:46 NKJV)

It doesn't matter that things may seem awful, terrible, hopeless, bleak, and not working out as you hope; you may feel lousy. If your heart condemns you and tells you that you have fallen into darkness, be assured that you are not in the dark when you are in Christ. In Him, you have His light, hope, and solution. He is the light in any area of darkness; He brings His light and hope and lifts the darkness of confusion, failure, fear, hopelessness, and helplessness.

He loves you and has given you His light so that you can walk with Him in love, joy, peace, and victory, overcoming sin and temptation. Jesus has conquered the darkness in the world and brought His everlasting light and peace, and you are in His light. Rejoice.

We have seen God's faithfulness over and over. When people believe God, trust Him completely, and are willing to rest in Him, they come out from the dark, and their lives are set on a more glorious course.

You are in His light, and you shall surely grow from glory to glory, regardless of what you are faced with today. Know that things cannot continue to go against you. As you keep your eyes on Jesus and continue to rest in Him, victory shall manifest soon. Stay confident in our Lord Jesus, knowing that He is fighting on your behalf and you shall surely overcome. Keep your eyes on Jesus, praise Him, honour Him, and glorify Him because He is your light.

> Thank You, Lord Jesus, for dying on the cross for me. I invite
> You to be Lord and Master of every area of my life. Help
> me to yield to You. I thank You that I can leave my cares
> and challenges with You, knowing that You are willing and
> able to handle them for me. I thank You, Jesus, and I receive
> Your light, peace, joy, healing, provision, and victory. Amen.

Day 56—In Christ, You Walk in Newness of Life

> Therefore we were buried with Him through baptism into death, that just as Christ was raised from the dead by the glory of the Father, even so we also should walk in newness of life. (Romans 6:4 NKJV)

When you invited Jesus to be the Lord and Master of your life, your old self died with Him at the cross, and you rose to new life with Him. You became born again. You ask, 'What new life do I have? I still have the same old challenges—those problems did not just disappear. I still get angry, fearful, and anxious. Those work problems still plague me, and those same relationship issues persist.'

The difference is that you now have the Spirit of the living God, the Spirit of Jesus in you. His Spirit of love, peace, joy, power and ability to overcome now lives in you, giving you victory in areas of your life where you yield to Him. The old, negative, defeated ways of living and thinking are things of the past. The enemy has no more power to defeat you. You have something new, divine and wonderful in you!

You can now walk with a clear mind, able to receive divine help and flourish in the solutions He brings. You have His ability to overcome weaknesses and thrive in His love and provision and live a life that reflects His glory and goodness. How awesome is that!

The key to walking in this new life is to embrace the truth that Jesus now lives in you through His Spirit. Take time, come to Him often. Feed on the Word of God. Keep growing in knowledge and relationship with Him. Spend time with Him, bask in His presence and love and receive His peace and joy. He too desires your fellowship. It brings Him joy and delight when you spend time with Him and when He sees you enjoying the benefits of His finished work and inheritance that is now yours. Be filled with Him and keep growing and glowing in His glory. Take time now to be with Jesus.

Day 57—You Are a New Creation in Him

> Therefore, if anyone is in Christ, he is a new creation; old things have passed away; behold, all things have become new. (2 Corinthians 5:17 NKJV)

When you became born again, your spirit became a new creation. But your thought life, emotions, and body have not been renewed. That's why you still dwell on wrong thoughts that do not align with your spiritual reality. Are thoughts of your family's history still bothering you? In your family, is there a history of broken marriages, early deaths, and inability to excel in careers and life? Are these making you fearful that you might suffer the same?

Praise Jesus that you are now a new creation in Him. Old things have passed away. Those negative problems in your family line have been cut off from you. God loves you so much and paid a high cost to set you free from bondage to the past so that you can walk in total freedom, fulfilling all the wonderful plans that He has for you.

We know a brother whose men in his family had a history of heart problems and early death. His great-grandfather, grandfather, father, uncles, and older brothers all died of heart problems by their late forties. When he was in his early forties he started to fear the same fate for himself. This was when he came to know Jesus as His Lord and Saviour. One day he read this verse that he had become a new creation in Christ and old things had passed away; all things became new. He received this and would tell himself daily that he was a new creation in Christ, and all things had become new. He continued to grow in the Lord, receiving these truths, and today he is in his seventies, has a successful business, and is still active in the church that he helped start.

Tell yourself daily that you are a new creation in Christ. Put your hand to your heart and say, "I am a new creation in Christ, set free from the old things of the past, in my life and in my family line. Thank You Jesus that You have made all things new and good for me. Amen"

Day 58—Walking as a New Creation

> For in Christ Jesus neither circumcision nor uncircumcision
> avails anything, but a new creation. (Galatians 6:15 NKJV)

When we believe Jesus as our Lord and Saviour, our old self—frightened, fearful, angry, anxious, unkind, unloving, rebellious and out of control, egoistic, prideful (dominated by the devil)—died with Him at the cross. We became a new creation in Christ, righteous, holy, pure, and precious in God's sight. You become set free to enter into all the possibilities and potential our heavenly Father has for you.

Life with Jesus is not about a list of things to do or not to do. It is living a life in relationship with the Creator. It's living life feeding on His love and goodness, and set free from depression, sicknesses, anxiety, fear, rebellion, and anger. It's about being the new person He made us, living in His love, peace, joy, favour, healing, provision, and blessings and shining His light to the world.

Your spirit has been wonderfully recreated in Christ. You have become a new creation, born of the Spirit. Therefore whenever you fall back to the old ways of complaints, fears, anxieties, anger, and depression, lift your eyes to Jesus. See His love and grace for you, and remind yourself that in Him. you are a new creation. Then walk in boldness in who you are in Him; an overcomer, deeply loved, full of His joy, peace, patience, kindness, hope and divine health.

Take time to thank and appreciate Jesus for giving you this new life in Him. See His face, His love, and peace. Enjoy and bask in His presence and love.

> Lord Jesus, thank You for Your wonderful gift of life. Thank
> You that I can walk in Your love, joy, peace, favour and blessings
> not because of anything I have done but simply because of Your
> love and sacrifice for me. Give me more revelation of Your
> wonderful love and grace. Teach me to know how to keep
> receiving Your love, peace, joy and life. Amen.

Day 59—He Is a Wonderful Counsellor and Prince of Peace

> For unto us a Child is born, Unto us a Son is given; And the government will be upon His shoulder. And His name will be called Wonderful Counselor, Mighty God, Everlasting Father, Prince of Peace. (Isaiah 9:6 NKJV)

The name Jesus means Son of God, Saviour of mankind, God is salvation, God incarnate, the Anointed One. Jesus is also called Wonderful Counsellor, Mighty God, Everlasting Father, and Prince of Peace. What a glorious Name. He is a merciful, loving and kind God who takes away our sin, sets us free from condemnation, guilt and shame and brings us His divine peace, guidance and comfort.

He is the Prince of Peace - He alone is our peace. The world may be shaken with all kinds of evil, yet we continue to enjoy His divine peace. But you say, "I am troubled and worried about so many things." Beloved, are you preoccupied with the issues of the day or are you preoccupied with Jesus? Start to choose Jesus, read the Word, meditate on His promises and let Him keep you in His perfect peace. As you look to Him, you position yourself to receive His comfort and counsel, leading and guiding you to paths of safety and security, joy, peace, prospering in all areas of your life.

Step out in faith and trust because when you depend on Him, He protects and shields you with His divine peace, keeping your heart strong. He is Wonderful Counsellor, Mighty God who enables you to overcome life's challenges and remain triumphant and victorious in the face of trials. He is truly our everlasting good Father!

> Thank You Jesus that You are my wonderful Counsellor, my peace, my mighty God and because of You I need not fear what goes on in the world but I can stand in faith and peace. Fill my heart with your light. Help me to always look to You to receive Your peace, guidance and counsel. Amen.

Day 60—You Are Transformed as You Behold Jesus

> But we all, with unveiled face, beholding as in a mirror the glory of the Lord, are being transformed into the same image from glory to glory, just as by the Spirit of The Lord.
> (2 Corinthians 3:18 NKJV)

As believers we have a tendency to judge ourselves and others for falling short. The world too, expects exemplary behaviour from Christians. The truth is that true transformation does not happen by our trying to do good and be good. It happens when we start beholding Jesus, looking at Him, fixing our gaze on Him.

No amount of will power or mental strength can cause us to change ourselves or save ourselves from sin, sickness, and consuming emotions like fear and anger, depression, bondages and destructive habits that ruin our lives and those we love. Neither can we try to be kind, patient, good, gracious and compassionate by our own will power. But when we turn to behold Jesus, His love and His wonderful finished work, His Spirit does the work of transforming us to become like Him. His Spirit supernaturally strengthens us, lifts us from fear and depression, sets us free from destructive bondages. His Spirit changes us to become compassionate, patient, kind and forgiving.

Therefore keep encouraging one another to behold Jesus. Keep pointing to Jesus, not to our sins, shortcomings, and failures. We can't save or transform ourselves. But as we behold Jesus, the Spirit does the work of transforming us to be like Him.

> Thank You, Lord Jesus for Your sacrifice and for the gift of the Holy Spirit. I submit to You areas of weaknesses – help me to see You in these weak areas, to see Your strength, Your love, Your beauty, Your peace that I might be transformed to become more and more like You in every way. Amen.

Day 61—From Hands That Killed to Hands That Grew Flowers

> Hope in the Lord; For with the Lord there is mercy, And with Him is abundant redemption. (Psalms 130:7 NKJV)

Do not be discouraged when life seems to come against you. When things look difficult, when you are challenged to compromise like the world, and when you are tired and there seems no way, take heart. You can totally depend on Jesus and His obedience and faithfulness. In Him, we come freely into the abundant redemption that our Father has for us and the abundance of His love and grace.

We know a brother whose family migrated to a Western country when he was young. He got involved with violent gangs and ended up in prison. While serving life imprisonment, he came to know Jesus and was transformed; he was no longer angry and aggressive. The officers took note, and his sentence was reduced from life to years. Months later, they decided to release him on condition that he returned to his birth country. There, we met him when he came to Bible school. His release was a miracle, but God had more for him.

We saw him struggle with a new language and adjusting to a new life, unsure of his future. Many times he was discouraged and wanted to give up, but he kept looking to Jesus, kept growing in the Word, and kept trusting Him. Six years later, we met him again and heard a most amazing testimony of God's abundant redemption. He now had a beautiful family and owned a thriving flower farm. He shared how God led Him and caused him to thrive. His wife read and taught him about planting flowers; land became available at the right time. Good customers came along. His farm took off, and he employed other ex-prisoners. Today, his greatest desire is to share the goodness, love and faithfulness of Christ with everyone he meets.

Only God can transform hands that killed into hands that cause flowers to flourish. God's redemption is abundant when we continue to trust Him. He can do for you too when you come to Him and trust Him completely.

Day 62—You Continue to Grow by the Grace of God

> Therefore, having been justified by faith, we have peace with God through our Lord Jesus Christ, through whom also we have access by faith into this grace in which we stand, and rejoice in hope of the glory of God. (Romans 5:1–2 NKJV)

Have you ever been sick, unemployed, anxious, or feeling totally defeated, and well-meaning friends told you that you had sin in your life, or that you had to go for this or that conference? Know the truth and be set free. You have been saved by grace, and God has given you the seed of faith to believe and receive His grace.

Grace is the unending, unconditional love that God has for us. He demonstrated His love by sending His Son, Jesus through whom we enter into His love, forgiveness, joy, peace, blessings and favour here on earth. These gifts have nothing to do with us, who we are, and what we have done. We are undeserving and it is because He is a loving and gracious God who desires to lavish us with His goodness.

Faith is our believing what God has done for us through Christ. It is faith that causes us to reach out and receive the grace of God. God has planted seeds of faith in us. When we exercise this faith, believing God, it enables us to receive the wonderful gifts of His love, joy, peace, favour, healing and blessed life that Jesus has for us.

Therefore do not get trapped into maintaining a list of things to do. Simply believe Jesus, keep coming to Him to receive His love and grace afresh. When you are anxious and fearful, exercise your faith and come back to Jesus, spend time in His presence, and bask in His love. Receive freely from Him and rejoice till you are full of Him.

Take time now and thank Jesus for all He has done for you. Recall the times you experienced His love and peace and tell Him how much you appreciate Him. Bask in His presence and let His love, joy, peace fill your heart.

Day 63—Look To The Lord Always

> In all your ways acknowledge Him, And He shall direct your paths. (Proverbs 3:6 NKJV)

As believers sometimes we put more trust in other things than Jesus. Perhaps you are more focused on your theology, clever thoughts and ideas, intelligence, or opinions? Or perhaps your trust and confidence is in your bank account, business, career, employer, the economy, your looks, or your friends? But all these are temporal, with no eternal value. Putting one's trust and confidence in these only causes us to be separated from the love and grace of our heavenly Father and the good path that He has for us.

God has much better for you than what the world can offer. Would you let go of your cleverness, strong opinions, trust in wealth, the economy or people and come to Jesus, acknowledging Him in all your ways? When you do that, He will lead you on a safe, secure, sound path; one that is filled with His peace, joy, wisdom, favour, wholeness, protection and provision.

What can I do to acknowledge Him? You can thank Him for what He did for you at the cross. You can dedicate time to read the Bible and learn about all that He has done for you. He has cleansed you of your sins, made you righteous, given you the gift of no condemnation, peace, joy, healing, protection, and every provision. Realise that every good thing that you have comes from Him. Know that He is always with you. Thank Him daily for everything – His protection, provision, peace, joy, and blessings.

When you take on this posture of acknowledging His presence with you and thanking Him in all your ways, you begin to quieten your own thoughts. And you begin to hear the still, small voice of the Holy Spirit more clearly within you. He is leading and guiding you to path of peace, joy and thriving in all areas of your lives. Take some time now, and thank Jesus and bask in His presence.

Day 64—God Created You for Himself

> This people I have formed for Myself; They shall declare My
> praise. (Isaiah 43:21 NKJV)

In the New Covenant, you and I are the people whom God has formed for Himself because we are in Christ. Jesus has died and made us new creations in Him. He is in us, and we are in Him. He formed us because He wants fellowship with us. He wants our companionship! That is the sole purpose of our lives: to be in fellowship and companionship with God, to praise and honour Him, and to live freely in the abundance that He has for us. We are God's own people, and He formed us for Himself.

What a glorious truth that our God formed us for Himself. We are not our own to do as we like. We are not our parents', not our spouse's, not our employers'. We are first and foremost God's children. We are formed for His pleasure, and His pleasure is to have us in relationship with Him, enjoying the fullness of His life.

If we belong to God, would God let anything come against us to harm us? No. The problem you are going through, the challenge, the pain, the sorrow—all these will pass. They are challenges for the moment, but soon His peace and joy will come back and keep you comforted and safe in His bosom.

If you are facing any challenge that seems insurmountable, know that God has made you for Himself. You belong to Him, and these challenges and trials are for a short time only.

Nothing pleases God more than when you come to Him because that's what He created you for—to be in relationship with Himself. So come to Him often, talk with Him, declare His praises and give thanks for His goodness and love. As you keep declaring praises and thanksgiving to Him, His Spirit within you releases His peace, joy, comfort, and hope. This is how you become restored. He has formed you, and His Spirit dwells within you, always ready to do good for you. Therefore, continue to come to Him always, giving Him praise and thanksgiving!

Day 65—He Heals the Broken-hearted

> He heals the broken hearted and binds up their wounds.
> (Psalm 147:3 NKJV)

Are you grieving, heartbroken, and in sorrow over a lost relationship, lost loved one, lost wealth, or lost health? No one else can truly understand your pain, but God does. He knows what you are going through.

Our heavenly Father is love, and He is merciful, gracious, and the source of all comfort. His heart and thoughts are of love for you, filled with good things towards you as any good father who desires the best for his children. Take heart. You are deeply loved by the Creator of this universe. He is love, He is the source of all comfort, and He desires to comfort you.

Even when you have failed and sinned, He is merciful, and His desire is to comfort you and let you see His love for you. Don't let your mistakes and failures keep you from coming to Him.

Come to Him with a sincere and humble heart, and He will heal you, bind up your wound and pain, and restore you. He wants to gather you in His arms and hug you and comfort you. He has already sent His beloved Son, Jesus, who suffered at the cross, taking your pains and sorrows upon Himself.

Jesus is with you right now and knows what you are going through. Let go and give Him your sorrows and pains. Let His peace and joy fill you.

Take this time and come to Jesus. Invite Him to sit with you. Let Him hug you and just rest in His presence. Enjoy the deep, abiding peace and calm and let it clear your heart, mind, and spirit.

> Thank You Lord Jesus for Your wonderful love for me. Thank You that You are my comfort and my peace. Thank You for Your presence with me. Fill me with Your shalom and be my strength. Amen.

Day 66—In Christ, Weeping Is for a Short Time

> For His anger is but for a moment, His favour is for life;
> Weeping may endure for a night, But joy comes in the
> morning. (Psalm 30:5)

Jesus came and at the cross, suffered all our heartaches, sorrows and anxieties, so He knows and understands the heartaches and sorrows that you go through. You are not alone in your suffering. He is there comforting and wiping away your tears. He is able to make all things right again for you. He already has a solution for your challenge.

His desire is for us to not succumb to these but to keep our eyes focussed heavenwards. He is the God of love, joy, and peace, and He alone can turn our sorrows into joyful dancing.

Jesus has risen from the dead and has also given us the victory over all our trials. Child of God Most High, you are dearly loved and accepted. Always remember that you are special and that He has you in the palm of His hands.

In the midst of troubles and trials, in the midst of sorrow, take comfort that this is only for a short while. Recall a time in the past where you were in deep sorrow but Jesus was there with you in your sorrow and joy came soon.

Let your thoughts dwell on Jesus and His love. See His love and goodness and see Him there with you, arms around you comforting you. Allow Him into your pain and sorrows. Share with Him and let Him lift you from sorrows into joyful dancing.

> Lord Jesus, I thank You for Your wonderful love for me. I
> know You are my Comfort who can restore peace and joy
> to me. Help me to surrender all my feelings and thoughts to
> You and to just rest in Your presence, in Your peace. Help
> me Lord especially when I am most weak and unable. Amen.

Day 67—He Lightens Your Load

> Take My yoke upon you, and learn from Me, for I am gentle
> and lowly in heart, and you will find rest for your souls.
> (Matthew 11:29 NJKV)

Are you tired of struggling in life, striving but never satisfied, trying hard but never achieving, comparing yourselves to others and feeling lousy, inadequate and condemned? As believers in this world, it is easy to forget our God is there for us and we go through life on our own strength and steam. When our eyes are not on God, it is easy to become tired, weary, worn out, burnt out, lonesome, and defeated.

God wants you to come to Jesus and rest in Him. He invites you to be yoked to Jesus and learn from Him. To become yoked with Jesus, we need to first become as He is, gentle and lowly in heart. In other words become humble, not full of ourselves, full of our own opinions, ideas and thinking. As we humble ourselves and let Him, we become yoked with Him and He bears our load and lightens things up for us. His yoke is light; He will never place a heavy burden on you.

He desires to prosper you in everything, whether it is your family, relationships, work, business, ministry, finances, health, etc. Yielded and yoked to Him, you align with His gentle thoughts and ways, and burdens become lifted. Worries and fears that used to weigh you down are lifted. He is able to cause things to work out in your favour because He loves you and has only good thoughts towards you.

Therefore quiet your thoughts and come to Jesus. He loves you. He is gentle, loving, kind, forgiving, and accepting. He is peace and joy, and He is able to do all things well for you. As you yield to Him and take upon yourself His gentleness and lowliness, you start resting in Him, and the things of this world lose its grip on you. Instead His love, joy, and peace radiate out of you as you rest from struggling in life and enjoying His blessed presence, His help and blessings.

Day 68—Jesus, the Word of God, Brings Us Life and Health

> The Word of God … 'is life to those who find them, and health to all their flesh.' (Proverbs 4:22 NKJV)

Sickness and disease were never part of God's plan for mankind. Adam was meant to thrive in good health in Eden. But sin led to sickness, disease, and eventually death. God's plan is for all mankind to live in good health, partaking fully of the abundant life that He has for us. Since Adam's fall, sickness and disease have become a part of this world, plaguing all of us at some point in our lives. In every society, medical care is a major cost and concern.

Sicknesses and the cost of treatment bring on anxieties, robbing us of the joy and fullness of life that God meant for us to enjoy. Sickness is an enemy of God. As a good Father, He has no desire for you His beloved child to be sick, diseased, suffering, anxious, and defeated. His wants to see you healed, well and living a glorious, thriving life.

Today's scripture tells us that the Word of God is life to those who find them and health to all their souls. He gave us Jesus, the Word of God. In Him is divine and supernatural healing! In His love and goodness, God has made provision for our healing by giving us Jesus, fulfilling what Psalm 107:20 says "He shall send forth His Word and heal us."

The verse in Mark 7:27 tells us that healing is the children's bread. It is God's basic provision for us because we are in Christ. Know and believe it is God's desire to heal you. Jesus went to the cross to set you free from sin but His body was also broken for your healing. Start to see Jesus as your Healer. Start to receive your healing, and see yourself healed and well because of Him.

> Thank You, Lord Jesus that You are the Word of God that brings healing, health and wholeness. Help me to keep an open heart to see that You are the Healer and that in You lies God's supernatural healing for me and my loved ones. Amen.

Day 69—God Wants to Heal You

> Who Himself bore our sins in His own body on the tree,
> that we, having died to sins, might live for righteousness—
> by whose stripes you were healed. (1 Peter 2:24 NKJV)

> Then the LORD said to Moses, "Make a fiery *serpent,* and set
> it on a pole; and it shall be that everyone who is bitten, when
> he looks at it, shall live." (Numbers 21:8 NKJV)

> And as Moses lifted up the serpent in the wilderness, even
> so must the Son of Man be lifted up. (John 3:14)

Jesus did not just give us eternal life but also brought God's supernatural healing to us. Today's scripture is based on Isaiah 53:5 that tells us that by His stripes we are healed. He suffered all the way to Calvary, stricken and striped, absorbing all our pains and illnesses on Himself. In return He gives us divine healing and health.

In the Old Testament is an account of how the children of Israel complained against God and how God sent fiery serpents that bit the people and many died. God then instructed Moses to make a bronze serpent and lift it on a pole. When those who were bitten by the serpents gaze at this bronze serpent, they were healed and lived. That bronze serpent that Moses made was a picture of Jesus who was lifted up on the cross.

In our sicknesses and diseases, if we fix our gaze on Jesus, the Brazen Serpent that God has given us, we position ourselves to receive His divine healing.

When symptoms come against you, you can either be filled with fear and anxieties, continue to be filled with pride and disbelief or you can choose to believe God's promise, and see your healing on the broken body of Jesus, receive the healing He has given you and stay rested in Him for He is your healer.

But that does not mean you stop going to your doctor or stop taking medication. Doctors and medicine are all part of God's healing provision for the world. As you see your doctor, you continue to look to Jesus for your healing because He is the ultimate healer.

Continue to see Jesus's body at the cross, stricken and striped, taking your sickness and disease upon Himself and see yourself healed, well and restored because of His sacrifice for you. Find someone who believes likewise and who can agree with you in prayer for healing for yourself and your loved ones.

O LORD my God,
I cried out to You,
And You healed me.
Psalm 30:2

Day 70—Mercy, Peace, and Love Is Yours

Mercy, peace, and love be multiplied to you. (Jude 2 NKJV)

God's desire is to see us healthy, thriving and living in all the grace and glory that He has for us. When you come to Jesus, God's mercy, love, and peace are multiplied to you, including God's grace for every situation, challenge, and circumstance in your life and His peace for every storm and upheaval. His love, mercy, and peace keep your heart stable and bring restoration in any area that has been stolen from you. He multiplies grace and causes you to triumph and prosper in all that you do.

I know a sister who for many years was working with a secular organisation advocating abortions amongst refugee women. One day she became ill, and her condition worsened. Her organs malfunctioned till she was bedridden. Doctors didn't know the cause of her problem and had no cure. In desperation, she started listening to Christian messages. Through a message, she was reminded of Jesus's resurrection—a message she vaguely remembered from her childhood.

She desperately and boldly asked God to raise her from her sickbed so that she could go to church that Sunday. God did. She came back to the Lord and continued trusting Jesus for total healing. Within months, her healing and restoration was complete. She has turned from desperation to living her life filled with hope, joy, peace, and health. She was our student at Bible school. Today, she is completely well; healed, restored and sharing Christ with others. Praise Jesus for His love, peace, and mercy that bring redemption, healing, and restoration. Only He alone can so beautifully redeem a soul.

Lift your head and tell yourself that you are greatly loved. He's got you covered no matter how bad or impossible your problem is. Whatever sickness or trouble you are facing right now, come to Jesus and let His mercy and peace be multiplied in your situation. Let His grace fill you with His calm and peace and lift you above the storm. He is able to do mightily for you.

Day 71—We Are Surrounded by God's Favour

For You, O Lord, will bless the righteous; with favour You
will surround him as with a shield. (Psalm 5:12 NJKV)

Jesus has made you righteous through His finished work at the cross. There's
no way you can make yourself righteous. But simply rest in Jesus, knowing
that He alone, by His blood shed for you, has made you righteous

It is easy to be troubled by challenging situations and circumstances. A close
family member lose their jobs, business or home, or come down with a disease;
news of a new disease or epidemic or news of a downturn in the economy, or
upheavals in the political situation, can all affect us and affect our peace. It is
all too easy to be weighed down by the negative news of the world. I am sure
you can relate with this.

As God's beloved children, we have His resources to rise above all the negative
circumstances that come at us. We have Christ with us. Keep looking to
Him. See His love and favour surrounding you like a shield protecting you
from anything that could come against you and harm you. The world can
be shaken, but because you are in Him, you stand on sound solid ground.
Keeping yourself in His perfect peace and joy, you position yourself to keep
receiving His blessings.

Therefore when challenges come, stay strongly grounded by reminding
yourself that He loves you and gave His life for you. He cares about you and
wants to protect you against that which would steal your peace and joy. His
favour keeps on pouring on you, blessing you and causing you to thrive even
in challenging times. Keep looking to Him, He desires more than anything
to keep you in His perfect peace and joy, to shield you from any attacks or
fiery darts from the enemy.

Thank You Lord for giving me Your righteousness. Thank
You for Your love, peace, and joy. I surrender my heart,
mind, and my life to You. Saturate me with Your love and
presence and let Your favour surround me. Amen.

Day 72—Jesus Came to Give You a Rich and Satisfying Life

> The thief does not come except to steal, and to kill, and to destroy. I have come that they may have life, and that they may have it more abundantly. (John 10:10 NJKV)

The devil is the thief who steals, kills, and destroys every good thing that God has for us—our joy, peace, relationships, health, finances, careers, ministries, and homes. Jesus came, died and was resurrected, defeating the devil at the cross. Because of Jesus you have been given His abundant life—a life that is full of His peace and joy, a life that is rich and satisfying and victorious over the devil.

But you say, "My life is far from joyful, peaceful and I don't see any abundance." The more you come to Christ and depend on Him, the more you position yourself to stop the enemy from stealing, killing and destroying the abundance that God has for you.

The enemy steals, kills and destroys through his lies and deception. He gives suggestions and thoughts that lead you down a road that brings no peace, no joy but destruction. How many suicides happen because the devil put lies in people's minds and they didn't know how to resist him? How many divorces happen, homes destroyed because people entertained the devil's lying schemes and thoughts? How many live in bondage to drugs, alcohol, pornography because the devil took advantage of their weaknesses and gave suggestions that led to their bondage, crippling them from living out their full potential? So many more problems are the result of the devil's blatant lies and man's ignorance and inability to counter these lies.

But he cannot prevail against the knowledge and power of God's love and truth. You are in Christ and you abound in His love, peace, joy, perfection and beauty. You can recognise the lies of the devil and you are in a position to resist him by replacing his lying thoughts with God's promises and truths.

When he lies to you that all is lost and gone, you tell him that Jesus is working things out. When he lies to you that God is ashamed of your past, you remind him that Jesus died and cleansed your past completely and God loves you as dearly as He loves Jesus. When he prompts you with thoughts that make you uncomfortable, tell him to be gone, that he has no place in you because you are a child of God.

> Lord Jesus, help me to keep my eyes and thoughts on You always. Thank You that I have Your wisdom to know and Your ability to resist the devil's lies and schemes. Help me to continue to abide in Your truth that I might live in the abundance of Your peace and joy. Amen.

The thief comes to steal, to kill, and to destroy. Jesus comes to give us abundant life.

Day 73—In Christ, Your Path Drips with Abundance

> You crown the year with Your goodness, And Your paths drip with abundance. (Psalm 65:11 NKJV)

If you are experiencing lack, if you are not seeing any good in your life, or if you are not experiencing joy and peace, do not feel condemned. The truth is that Jesus loves you and has made available to you His goodness and His abundance in all areas of your life.

The key is to stay focussed on Jesus. He wants fellowship with you, and He wants you coming to Him freely, with joy and an open heart, just as a natural father would love his child to come to him.

Are there grumblings and complaining in your heart? Is there envy in your heart? Are there fears and dread in your heart? Is there a spirit of hopelessness within you? Are you looking at every lack, every bad, every challenge and struggle—and magnifying them? Are you filled with self-pity, allowing sadness to engulf you because you think you are a victim of life's circumstances?

Are you willing to stop grumbling and complaining and start appreciating all the blessings in your life, no matter how small, thanking Jesus for these blessings?

Instead of being envious, will you start to rejoice with others for their blessings? Will you lift your eyes to God and thank Him that He has so much to give to all of us. He always has more for everyone. Are you willing to come to Jesus, spend time with Him, and receive His love and joy? Will you replace that dread, fear, and self-pity in your heart with a sense of His great love for you and all that He is to you?

Come to Jesus, bask in His love, and let His peace fill your heart. Open your heart to His love. He loves you greatly and desires to fill you with all abundance of His peace, joy, favour, blessings. Start to see yourself greatly loved, see yourself enjoying His favour and blessings.

Day 74—Let Your Soul Delight in Abundance

> Listen carefully to Me, and eat what is good, And let your
> soul delight itself in abundance. (Isaiah 55:2b NKJV)

We are bombarded with a varied choice of entertainment and feeding through the news and social media. All kinds of religious and philosophical thoughts, teachings on exercises, diets, and how to live right, abound. Others try to show you how to get on top of things. These bring you man's own ideas, values, and thoughts about life. We live in this world and cannot avoid this bombardment of information. But God has something better for us.

God desires for us to feed on what will cause our soul to delight in His abundance. He made you wonderfully in His image, and He knows what will make you thrive in abundance: feeding on Christ.

What does it mean to feed on the Lord Jesus? Read and meditate on His finished work for you. Feeding on His Word, His truth, and His love for you is the key to your soul delighting itself in abundance. God knows that any other thing we feed on, apart from Jesus, cannot fulfil that deep longing within each person for truth, for love, and for real acceptance and belonging. Feeding on Christ builds in you a deep sense of His love and acceptance for you. It builds a strong connectedness with your Creator; soothes all the insecurities and fears; keeps you in His love, peace, and joy; and keeps your soul delighting in His abundance.

But you find yourself spending hours on Facebook, watching video after video. You say, 'I am so addicted. How do I get out?' Firstly, there's no condemnation if you are in this situation. Even as you are watching a video, be conscious of Jesus right there with you. Tell Him how much you appreciate all that He has done for you. Keep on turning your thoughts to Him. Sometimes you simply have to say no to that computer or TV and consciously turn to Jesus! Keep on doing that daily, and soon you develop a lifestyle of abiding by and feeding on Jesus. Fears, worries, and anxieties will soon have no place in you, because you will know how to turn to Jesus and delight in the abundance that God has for you.

Day 75—You Will Prosper in All Things

> Beloved, I pray that you prosper in all things and be in health, just as your soul prospers. (3 John 2 NKJV)

Our heavenly Father loves us dearly, and He desires for us to be well and thriving in every area of our life, our health, our emotions, our thinking, our plans, and our relationships. He has made it possible through His Son, Jesus, through whom the Holy Spirit has been given to us to lead us into all the good things that He has for us.

Calamities, sicknesses, and diseases, all kinds of problems may come against us, and everything seems not right. It may be so difficult to make sense of what's going on. We may even wonder where God is.

He is right there in your every tear, in your every question, in your every doubt, in your every sorrow and pain, and in your weariness. When evil comes against you, Jesus is right there with you. Sometimes the mind may scream something else, but quieten yourself, and in that still small voice, you will hear His love, His assurance, His shalom, and His joy.

He wants you to prosper in your soul! Start to see His love for you, visualize what it is like to walk in His peace, joy, protection, favour and blessings. Especially in the midst of the worse calamity, do not succumb to fear or be shaken. Instead see Him holding you up. See His protection and favour covering you. Remind yourself that He desires for you to prosper in your soul and in everything else because when you prosper in your soul, the enemy loses his power over you.

When you prosper in your soul, any trial, challenge that the enemy throws at you becomes an opportunity for you to grow in greater abundance of God's love, grace, peace and joy. Stay focussed on Jesus and walk in the help and blessings He has for you. You are indeed deeply loved and God's hand is on you. Take time to thank and praise Jesus for all that He has done for you.

Day 76—Do Not Worry

> Therefore do not worry about tomorrow, for tomorrow will
> worry about itself. Each day has enough trouble of its own.
> (Matthew 6:34 NKJV)

When we worry, we allow the enemy to steal our peace and joy. God, in His wisdom and infinite love, gives us so many instructions about not worrying. He does so because through His Son, Jesus, He has already made every provision for all that we need in this life.

He has commanded His angels to keep watch over us, protecting us. He has already made that provision of a job, of a position to meet all our material needs. He has made provision of fellowship and companionship so that we are connected and never isolated. He has made provision of family so we enjoy acceptance and love. He has made provision of healing so that we are well. In the face of all the problems the world is in, His promises hold true for us because we are His beloved children. We stand on solid ground because He is our God who loves us and cares for us.

On the other hand, worrying causes us to become fearful and fretful, to lose our peace and joy—the very gifts that God wants us to enjoy—and blocks the flow of every provision, healing, favour, and blessing that God has for us.

Therefore, do not worry. Focus instead on the extent of the love of God for you. Meditate on how awesome, how mighty, how merciful and gracious He is. Focus on all that Jesus did for you at the cross. When you do so, your soul rejoices, and you allow God's favour, blessings, and provision to flow unblocked into your life.

> Thank You dear heavenly Father for Your love and provision
> for me. Thank You that You have already supplied all that I
> need, all that my family needs. Draw me to continually look
> to You for every area of need in my life. Amen.

Day 77—Take Heart, Parents; He Knows Your Challenges

> He will gather the lambs with His arm, And carry them
> in His bosom, And gently lead those who are with young.
> (Isaiah 40:11 NKJV)

As a parent, you face many challenges in bringing up your children. You see your children becoming rebellious and strong-headed, rejecting your values and counsel, and you feel inadequate, hurt, and anxious, not knowing how to guide them.

Be comforted because Jesus knows what you are going through. He knows the responsibilities and challenges that you have in bringing up your child. He does not want you stressed, anxious, or blaming yourself when you see your child become rebellious. He desires to guide you, comfort you, and draw you close to His bosom to encounter His warm, assuring, comforting presence and quell all those fears, anxieties, pain, and heartaches. In His abundant love and comfort, He wants you to realise that He is also the shepherd of your child and that He loves your child more than you ever could.

We know parents who were concerned and worried about their children, especially in their teenage years. We have countless testimonies of parents who stayed close to the Lord, committing their children to Him in prayers, and how their children turned out to become responsible young men and women.

Do not be anxious about your children. Instead, draw close to the Lord and hear His heart for you. See His power and ability that He desires to use on your behalf. He desires to gather not just you but your child to Himself, to His heart, to keep you safe, secure, comforted, and rested in Him, enjoying all the goodness that He has for you. Open your heart and receive His love and guidance.

Take time to praise and thank Jesus for His sacrifice and that His goodness and love is not just for you but for your children and other loved ones too.

Day 78—Your Own Mistakes Cannot Separate You from the Love of Christ

> Who shall separate us from the love of Christ? Shall tribulation, or distress, or persecution, or famine, or nakedness, or peril, or sword? (Romans 8:35 NKJV)

Sometimes we create our own problems because we are stubborn, headstrong, and rebellious. When we know we have been responsible for creating our own problems, we may think that there is no way God will help us. Have you felt this way before? How far from the truth!

Because of the finished work of Christ at the cross, you are today seated with Him at the right hand of the Father. In Christ, the Father loves you; nothing can separate you from His love. His grace is abounding to you. If you have lost something because of your mistakes: relationships, finances, opportunities, or health, rest assured that He can and is willing to restore to you what you have lost. That is how dearly your heavenly Father loves you.

No trial, tribulation, distress, persecution, famine, danger, or calamity of any kind, not even death, can cause us to be separated from the love that the Father has for us. No mistake of your own can also cause you to be separated from your heavenly Father.

Turn your eyes to your heavenly Father. See His gentle love towards you. Stop looking at yourself and your failures, mistakes, and weaknesses. See instead the extent of His love for you. He does not condemn you. He sent you Jesus, and His love for you is eternal. Receive His love afresh right now. Take a deep breath, receive His love, His forgiveness and let it fill your heart with peace and joy. Come to your Father; He awaits you.

> Thank You, heavenly Father, for Your wonderful love for me even though I am undeserving. Thank You for Your goodness and grace. Amen.

Day 79—You Are the Precious Treasure That God Sought

> The kingdom of heaven is like treasure hidden in a field,
> which a man found and hid; and for joy sells all that he has
> and buys that field. (Matthew 13:44 NKJV)

While growing up, I thought that Jesus was the treasure in the field, and I, the merchant that found Him and sold everything to buy Him. Did you also have that same mistaken thought? As I understood the grace of God, my eyes were opened. I saw that I am the treasure hidden in the field and the man that went and sold everything to buy me is Jesus. That set me free from a terrible burden, knowing that I could never do anything to purchase Jesus.

There is nothing you could do to earn His love, acceptance, and blessings, nothing you could do to 'purchase' Him. The kingdom of heaven is all about what Jesus did: He gave up the majesty and splendour of heaven to come into our rottenness, and He purchased us for Himself.

Start seeing yourself as that precious treasure that Jesus bought for Himself and for His Father. That is how much God loves you, and that is how He sees you: a precious treasure that He sent His beloved Son to redeem.

You may not be used to thinking of yourself as a precious treasure but God wants you to renew your mind according to His Word, according to how He sees you. Therefore when negative thoughts about yourself arise, remember you are a precious treasure to God. Replace those negative thoughts and meditate on all that Jesus did for you. The truth is that you are greatly loved and precious to Him and you belong to Him. How wonderful to belong to God and have His love, fellowship, peace, joy, protection and every good thing for eternity!

> Dear Jesus, open the eyes of my understanding. Let me see
> more and more Your great love for me. Help me receive
> Your love. Lead me to walk in the fullness of everything my
> heavenly Father has for me, and transform me to live my life
> for Your glory. Amen.

Day 80—God Has Precious Thoughts of You

> How precious are your thoughts about me, O God. They cannot be numbered. I can't even count them; they outnumber the grains of sand. And when I wake up, you are still with me. (Psalm 139:17–18 NLT)

This Psalm reminds us that God has wonderful, precious thoughts towards us. He loves you and me and thinks about us day and night. What an awesome thought; that we occupy so much of God's mind and heart! The number of His thoughts of us is much more than the grains of sand. This is how precious you are to Him.

People may betray us, speak wrongfully about us, bear false witness against us, and we are not in a position to defend ourselves. Have you been in this situation? Or experiencing this right now? Know that God knows exactly what you are going through. It is natural to be concerned about what others think of us and what a lousy feeling to suffer a betrayal. But be assured that God's heart and thoughts are with you. He only has good thoughts of you. When you know how much God loves you, it becomes easier to bless people for the wrong they do to you.

So in the midst of the pain of betrayal, turn your heart to bless those who hurt you and keep your peace in Christ. God will defend you. He can cause all that is said to fall on deaf ears so that no damage is done to you. He can continue to promote you and honour you in the presence of others.

God has good thoughts towards you. No matter what other challenge may come against you, keep seeing His love for you. He is right there in the midst of your tears and fears and He doesn't think any worse of you. Take heart, you are truly precious to God.

> Help me heavenly Father, to grasp what it means that You think precious thoughts of me, so much these thoughts outnumber the grains of sand. Thank You for Your love for me and I love You, dear heavenly Father. Amen

Day 81—Be Rooted in His Love

> He would grant you, according to the riches of His glory, to be strengthened with might through His Spirit in the inner man that Christ may dwell in your hearts through faith; that you, being rooted and grounded in love. (Ephesians 3:16–17 NKJV)

Are you struggling with loneliness, feeling neglected, rejected, and unloved? Or maybe you just had a spat with family or friends and are feeling isolated and unappreciated? Know that Jesus loves you very dearly. He is right there with you. He wants to comfort and strengthen you and set you free to receive His joy and peace and dwell in it.

No matter what others say or the thoughts and feelings you have, the truth is God loves you deeply and dearly. You are precious to Him and He loves you more than you realise. He wants you so strongly grounded in the truth of His love for you because that is how you are strengthened in your inner being.

Open your heart to dwell on how much Jesus loves you and what He did for you at the cross. He wants to take your weariness and lift you into a place of rejoicing. When you put your trust in Him and the love that He has for you, you find yourself being lifted. Therefore be deeply rooted in Christ's love and His presence with you and no matter who may come against you, His Spirit will keep you in His peace.

Dwell on His great love for you instead of thinking nobody cares about you. Open your arms and praise Him and allow the power of the Holy Spirit to lift and comfort you. Before you know it, you find yourself forgiving those who offended, neglected, and rejected you and your heart flooded with His love.

> Thank You, heavenly Father, that You sent Your beloved Son, Jesus, for me. Thank You for Your love for me. Help me to always look to You, draw on Your love for me, and strengthen my inner being. I praise and glorify You, Jesus. Amen.

Day 82—God Will Always Do Good for You

> I will make an everlasting covenant with them: I will never
> stop doing good for them. I will put a desire in their hearts
> to worship me, and they will never leave me. (Jeremiah
> 32:40 NLT)

Throughout the Old Testament, God made covenants with the Old Testament saints, who were mere men, because He wanted to set them apart and pour His fullness into them. God's promise that He would make an everlasting covenant with His people was fulfilled by Jesus at the cross.

In a covenant, what belongs to one party now also belongs to the other. Therefore through the everlasting covenant of the blood of Jesus, God absorbed all our brokenness, pain, suffering, sicknesses, diseases, lack, and curses. In turn, what is God's is now ours: glory, love, peace, joy, goodness, kindness, abilities, powers, protection, abundant provision, and blessings.

This is the wonderful, everlasting covenant that God entered into with Jesus. It is eternal, unchangeable, and unshakeable, and it's entered into completely for our benefit. Jesus, our covenant partner, now fights our battles and steps in to do good for us all the time.

This is His magnificent way to ensure you know He will never stop doing good for you. He wants you to enter into the fullness of life that He has for you.

It has nothing to do with what we have or have not done. God the Father and God the Son made this everlasting covenant simply because He loves us and desires to do good for us. Do not fret when things seem to be against you, when challenges and trials happen. Have total confidence that God is doing good for you right now and will never stop being good to you.

Take time to thank your heavenly Father for this Covenant with Jesus to bring you His protection, provision, healing and every blessing.

Day 83—Believe, and You Will Start Seeing the Goodness of God

> Does God give you the Holy Spirit and work miracles among you because you obey the law? Of course not. It is because you believe the message you heard about Christ. (Galatians 3:5 NLT)

God is the one who supplies His Spirit to us, works miracles amongst us, and blesses us beyond what we can think or imagine. We walk in His miracles and blessings not because God is impressed by our good works, and not because of our prayers, our Bible reading, or our charitable works. We walk in them simply because we believe and trust in Jesus and His finished work.

Whenever we look to Jesus and put our trust in Him, casting our cares on Him and resting in Him, God's Spirit works to supply us in every area of need, supplying the miracle that we need, be it finance, healing, relationship, or restoring us to wholeness, so that we reflect His glory and grace.

The only part we need to do is believe. Don't wait to see before you believe. But believe, rest in Him, leave all the fears and anxieties to Him, and start seeing His love, peace, joy, hope, healing, favour, and blessings. Believe and see with your spiritual eyes His favour abounding on you and doors open for you. See new opportunities come along, and those bad symptoms gone. See challenging situations become miraculously resolved, and things work out beautifully beyond your understanding.

When you hear and believe, and your heart yields to Christ, you let God's Spirit work in you, supplying abundantly all that you need. God wants you to walk in the fullness of all that He has for you. Believe in Jesus, trust Him, cast your cares on Him, rest in His love for you, and walk in His light and glory.

Do not wait to see before you believe. But believe with your heart and start to see God's goodness.

Day 84—The Spirit Lets Us Know We Are God's Children

> The Spirit Himself bears witness with our spirit that we are children of God. (Romans 8:16 NKJV)

A father-son relationship speaks of a special bond, especially between a good father and his son. A good father loves, protects, affirms and encourages his child. He builds a good relationship with his child, looks out for him and supports him to become the best he can be. A child with a good father feels loved, secure, and protected; he feels whole.

God's desire is for you to know that He is a good heavenly Father who loves you dearly, and that He is never too busy for you. You can totally depend on Him to protect you, fight for you, provide for you, and do everything a good father does.

He wants us to know that as His children, we have a special privileged bond with Him. The first thing the Holy Spirit does when we come to Jesus is witness to our spirits that we are indeed God's children. He wants us to know how special we are to Him, how well loved we are, and how He's looking out for us as a good father would.

As we quieten the noises around us and focus on Jesus, the Holy Spirit's promptings become clearer to us. Listen to the Holy Spirit. In the midst of the issues and troubles of the day, He whispers to you that you are a child of the Most High God. He assures you that your identity is God's beloved child. He wants you to know that all His resources are available to you to live victoriously and gloriously. You lack nothing. You have no fear. You are never alone and never without help.

Lift your eyes off the challenges and trials. See yourself well loved, well supplied and well protected by your heavenly Father. All is fine with you because the Creator of this universe is your beloved heavenly Father who loves you and delights to give you His best. Amen.

Day 85—The Holy Spirit Will Testify of Jesus

> But when the Helper comes, whom I shall send to you from
> the Father, the Spirit of truth who proceeds from the Father,
> He will testify of Me. (John 15:26 NKJV)

The Helper, the Holy Spirit, the Spirit of truth lives in us today. He testifies of Jesus, bears witness, and reminds us of all that Jesus has done for us. He reminds us that Jesus died as our sin and gave us His righteousness. That He took our sicknesses upon Himself and made us well. That He was rich but became poor to make us rich. And He became a curse at the cross to set us free from the curse of the law and bring us God's blessings.

The Holy Spirit is always gently reminding you that you are a beloved child of God; loved, favoured, blessed, and healed. You're the apple of His eye, and you live under an open heaven because of the finished work of Jesus.

When you feel like you are not good enough, the Holy Spirit reminds you that in Christ, you are totally accepted, the Father loves you, and you are special and precious to Him. When symptoms come against your body, He reminds you that Jesus bore your sicknesses and diseases on His body at the cross.

When you are anxious about your finances, He reminds you that Jesus was rich but became poor at the cross to bring you the abundant provision of heaven. When life's challenges make you feel weak, He reminds you that in Christ, you are made strong. He reminds you that you can do all things in Christ who strengthens you. He reminds you that you indeed have the mind of Christ and are able to process and think like Him.

Keep reading the Word of God and renewing your thoughts and mind according to what God says about you. As you do so, it becomes easier for you to hear the Spirit's gentle promptings because He always leads you according to God's Word, to the good thoughts He has of you and to the overcoming life that is yours in Christ. May you be blessed by the fullness of God – by Father, Son and Holy Spirit!

Day 86—You Are Led by the Holy Spirit

> For as many as are led by the Spirit of God, these are sons of God. (Romans 8:14 NKJV)

In the New Covenant, we are no longer led by a set of laws like the Old Testament saints. Instead, the Holy Spirit dwells in believers, sanctifying us, leading and guiding us to the provision, protection, peace, and the paths that God has for us.

How does the Holy Spirit lead us? He speaks to our hearts, and gives us ideas about what to do and how. He is always leading, prodding us to the plans, purposes, and destiny that God has for us.

How do you position yourself to be led by the Holy Spirit? The more you look to Jesus, depend on Him and make Him the centre of your life, the more space you make for the Holy Spirit to move, for His leading and presence to become supernaturally natural to you.

Focusing on your challenges and circumstances, will only fill you with all kinds of fears and anxieties that prevent you from hearing the Holy Spirit's leading and His voice of peace, calm, love, and direction.

But stay focussed on Jesus, meditate on the Word and on His finished work, and you allow the Holy Spirit to fill you with His peace and joy. In that place of rest, the Holy Spirit's leading becomes clear to you. He wants to lift you from fears, fill you with joy, give you thoughts and ideas, prompt you what to do and whom to see and speak with. He may supernaturally remove a challenge or problem. His wants you flowing in the rhythm of God's abounding grace and love. Come to Him.

> Dear Holy Spirit, thank You for Your love for me. Thank You that You are always leading me and guiding me in the ways of God. I want more of You in my life, more guidance and leading in God's ways. Show me, teach me to hear more from You. Amen.

Day 87—You Are Filled With the Holy Spirit

> But Christ has blessed you with the Holy Spirit. Now the Spirit stays in you, and you don't need any teachers. The Spirit is truthful and teaches you everything. So stay one in your heart with Christ, just as the Spirit has taught you to do. (1 John 2:27 CEV)

As believers of Christ, we are vessels made for the Holy Spirit of God. When you invited Jesus into your life, you are in effect saying that you empty your life. You empty the old vessel so that He can fill you, bless you with His Spirit. As a Spirit-filled believer, you are constantly connected with God's Spirit and constantly receiving from Him. He is constantly teaching us the truths of God.

This scripture tells us to stay one in heart with Christ, who He is, and all that He has done for us because He is the way, the truth, and the life. The Holy Spirit is the same Spirit as Jesus; He is perfect love, peace, joy, and comfort, and He knows all things. They work together to strengthen us and bring us into the good paths God has for us.

The Holy Spirit brings illumination, enlightenment, and revelation of the truths of God. When we are one heart with Christ, trusting Him for what He has done for us at the cross, our spirits resonate in joy when we hear God's truths. That is the Holy Spirit in us responding in agreement. And when we hear a lie there is unease in our spirit. Continue to read and meditate on the Word, know God's heart because when you are of the same heart as Christ, you are in a position to continue to be taught by the Holy Spirit.

Therefore, let Jesus dwell in your heart. Fix your eyes on Him, look to Him always, and see His love, goodness, and kindness. Let His love, joy, peace, grace, compassion, healing, forgiveness, and provision fill your heart. In doing so, you are in a place to allow the Holy Spirit to take you to so much more that God has for you. Continue to dwell and meditate on this.

Day 88—You Have the Spirit of God, Not the Spirit of the World

> We have received, not the spirit of the world, but the Spirit who is from God, that we might know the things that have been freely given to us by God. (1 Corinthians 2:12 NKJV)

The spirit of the world speaks fear, worry, anxiety, lack, sickness, bondage and enslavement to destructive habits. It speaks negative and harasses you. It speaks cunning, scheming, and deceit. It speaks of selfish ambition, ego, pride and self-glory. It speaks destruction, damage and harm. Today, the spirit of the world is at work to confuse and pervert God's love. It boasts of a human love that accepts and condones sin. What is good and of God is touted as evil and what is evil to God is touted as good.

Child of God, you do not have the spirit of the world. When it tries to speak to you, do not receive from it. Through Christ, the Spirit of God lives in you and you know the good things that God has freely given to you. The Spirit of God speaks of beautiful, lovely and heavenly things. He speaks of son-ship, of a heavenly citizenship, of His love, forgiveness, acceptance, protection, provision, possibilities and satisfaction. He speaks His love, joy, peace, faith, clear mind, perfection and rest. He speaks of His sufficiency, abundant supplies and good plans for you. In Him there is no harm. He fights your battles, and you do not need to resort to what the world does.

Keep coming to God's Word. Know His love for you and His good and wonderful thoughts towards you. The more you know this, the more sensitive you are in your spirit to discern the delightful things that God has freely given you. He is a very generous Father who loves you very much and wants to give you good.

> Heavenly Father, thank You for Your wondrous love for me. And for Your Spirit who shows me all the things that You have freely given to me. Illumine my heart. Help me to be more sensitive to You so that I am able to discern what is of You and what is not. Amen.

Day 89—God Hears Us When We Ask According to His Will.

> Now this is the confidence that we have in Him, that if we ask anything according to His will, He hears us. (1 John 5:14 NKJV)

It's easy to forget that God is our help, and we get all worried, fearful, slogging hard, and getting tired, stressed and discouraged. When was the last time that you forgot to come to God and was anxiously trying to get things done by your own might? Or you were just so stressed out about a situation, forgetting God's help is just at hand. When we look to Jesus, trust Him, and know that His heart towards us is to see us thrive, He can do much more for us. He can drop ideas and suggestions and cause things to happen to bless us.

We have friends who own a vegetable wholesale business. For a time, the husband was lukewarm in his faith, and the couple struggled with the business. They were anxious in the face of increased orders and discouraged that they could not obtain financing. We reminded them of Jesus and His faithfulness and love. They chose to commit and trust in Jesus. His response to challenges was now, 'Let's trust Jesus.' One day while praying, the Lord reminded him of crowdfunding. A light bulb went off in his heart. He wrote a short pitch on his financing needs and sent it out to a few friends and relatives. Within hours, he received a response. A complete stranger received his pitch and wanted to invest the exact amount that they needed. That same night, the money was transferred to their account, and they were able to expand their business. Today they have a thriving business.

All we need is a word from the Lord. Just an idea from Him can give us the breakthrough we need. Stay focussed on Jesus, keep Him in the meditation of your heart and mind, and come to Him earnestly for every need. When we look to Jesus and focus on Him, we hear the guidance and leading of the Spirit more clearly and more surely, leading us to walk in victory, success, love, peace, joy, and every provision. God desires to see you thrive and succeed because He is a very good Father.

Day 90—God Is Faithful

> God is faithful, by whom you were called into the fellowship
> of His Son, Jesus Christ our Lord. (1 Corinthians 1:9 NKJV)

God is faithful, and we can totally depend on and trust Him. He has called us into fellowship with His Son, Jesus, our Lord. We can depend on Father, Son, and Holy Spirit, who dwells with us. God will not fail us nor forsake us. He is the constant help in our lives, the one we can depend on to lift us and restore us.

You may be in a situation where you feel insecure about your future. You have been without a job, and nothing seems to be opening up. You're running out of savings and are stressed and anxious.

I remember the time when a good friend was out of a job and stressed. The pressures from family did not help. During this time, she continued trusting the Lord. A couple of weeks later, a company that she had interviewed with a few months before called her. The position that was previously closed to her had reopened, and she was given the position.

God is faithful and able. When we come humbly before Him, He will never turn a deaf ear to our requests. He can cause a closed situation to be opened again and create that position for you. He can bless you beyond what you expect because He is not just your good Father, He is also God the Creator and all things are possible with Him.

Take time to refocus your thoughts. A temporary obstacle you face does not thwart God's good plans for your life. Bring your thoughts back to focus on God and on how faithful, kind, and dependable He is. He is your good, heavenly Father who wants to bless you and shower you with His favour, love, peace, joy; and to see you thrive. Look to Him earnestly in any need, challenge, or situation. Trust Him to deliver, protect, heal, provide, and bless you in every way because He is good and faithful

Day 91—Jesus Is Unchanging

> Jesus Christ is the same yesterday, today, and forever.
> (Hebrews 13:8 NKJV)

People change over time. They may favour you one day and change their mind the next. They may think the world of you and then change their minds because of something you did or did not do. Even close family does that.

Your wealth could be with you today, but you do not have complete assurance that it will stay safe with you forever. In economic downturns, people have lost the companies that they had spent their lives building. Jobs that once were thought secure are easily gone in bad times. Possessions like homes, cars, and other valuables can be easily lost. The economy and the stock market change constantly. One day it is up, and the next, it is down. Experts have been wrong in predicting the direction of the market. There is no way we can find our security here. We are not guaranteed forever with the people we love. Loved ones leave or die, and we are back on our own.

But what wonderful assurance we have that Jesus is always unchanging. His love for us never changes, and His esteem for us never changes. His forgiveness towards us never changes, regardless of what we have done or not done, or how we have failed. His grace towards us is constant, unaffected by our behaviour. His blessings continue to pour on us. His saving grace continues to pour out to the world regardless of how the world rejects Him.

Therefore let's look to Jesus, our beloved Saviour, for He alone can be trusted. He alone is constant—the same yesterday, today, and forever. Take time and praise Jesus for His wonderful love for you, for His sacrifice that has not just given you eternal life, but every help and provision that you need in this life. Thank Him for giving you joy and peace.

> Thank You, Lord Jesus that even thought I don't deserve it, Your love and commitment to me is always constant and unchanging. I appreciate how awesome You are, always faithful and good. I thank You and I love You. Amen.

Day 92—Are You Trusting Jesus, or Is Your Heart Filled with Fears?

> But blessed are those who trust in the LORD and have made the LORD their hope and confidence. (Jeremiah 17:7 NLT)

Jesus came to die for the world, yet not the whole world is blessed with all that He has done for us at the cross. Many in the world and in the Church are struggling with sickness, depression, lack, anger, addiction, broken relationships, and bad habits that destroy lives.

In this scripture, the Lord promises that those who trust in Him and put their hope and confidence in Him are blessed. He loves you and me. He is the Creator of the whole universe and of everything that exists. His desire is always for your good, for you to thrive. However, it is only by submitting and yielding to His leading that you can align with the wonderful blessings that He has for your life.

Are you putting your trust in Jesus and Jesus alone, or are you beset with fears, worries, and anxieties? Do you have an outward display of trusting Jesus, but in your heart you are chasing all ways and means, chasing one person after another, one project after another, to resolve your situation? Are you chasing prayer meeting after prayer meeting to get your healing, or are you truly resting in Jesus alone?

When you trust Jesus and put your hope and confidence in Him, you start resting in Him. He is patient, kind and forgiving. When you have spent your energies and have no more ideas or means left, come to Him. He welcomes you with open arms, ready to pour His love, peace, joy and blessings on you.

Spend time to read and meditate on His word and listen to His heartbeat. You will begin to hear His love, peace, calm, and wisdom, hear His plans and see with His eyes a wondrous and lovely path ahead lit by His love and light. Be patient and you soon start to walk in the good blessings that He has for you as you grow strong in His presence and filled with His peace.

Day 93—You Are Blessed with Every Spiritual Blessing in Christ

> Blessed be the God and Father of our Lord Jesus Christ, who
> has blessed us with every spiritual blessing in the heavenly
> places in Christ. (Ephesians 1:3 NKJV)

Your heavenly Father loves you and knows all your needs. He has already made every provision for you. Jesus came to bear our sin and our sicknesses, sorrows, and curses. In return He gave us His righteousness, peace and joy. The greatest blessing He gave us is being restored to a relationship with our heavenly Father. The wonderful fringe benefit of this relationship is that He gives us every other material blessing that we need to thrive in this life.

Years ago, after I sold my business, I became anxious about what to do next. In my anxiety, I started to read and meditate on the promises of God. I reminded myself that I was worthy. These promises became a soothing balm to my anxious mind. After a few months of doing that, opportunities started happening. I acted on a most unlikely suggestion, but it turned out to be God's wonderful blessing for five years of thriving and soul restoration.

Our Father's heart is to have a relationship with us. But He also wants to bless you. He knows your every need and He is able to supply them all. Stop focussing on the obstacles and challenges. Because that will only get you more worried and anxious. And worry and anxiety will only block you from receiving the blessings that He has for you.

Sometimes a person cannot receive because of feeling unworthy. Start to align your thinking with Christ's. He loves you, you are precious to Him and He sees you totally worthy and deserving. He wants to bless you, and establish you soundly on His love, peace and joy and give you good gifts. Therefore, see yourself totally worthy of His blessing.

Come to Jesus. Come to your heavenly Father. In the midst of your worry and anxiety, come to Him. When you come to Him, trusting Him, He will never disappoint you. He is a very good Father who loves you dearly. He will open doors for you and cause His blessings to come on you.

Day 94—The Lord's Blessings Come with No Sorrow

The blessing of the LORD makes one rich, And He adds no sorrow with it. (Proverbs 10:22 NJKV)

When God blesses us, there is no sorrow added. In contrast, the success of the world often comes with stress, backbiting, conniving, distrust, infidelity, unfaithfulness, lying and cheating that lead to broken relationships, broken homes, much pain and sorrow.

Not so for the blessings that come from God. It is purely by God's grace that we are first blessed to be righteous, forgiven, and adopted into His kingdom. He blesses you, blesses your home and adds no sorrow with it, as a good father would. He establishes us on a solid foundation of His perfect love and He tops off His blessings and favour on us with His goodness, love, joy, and peace.

If you are not experiencing the complete blessing of God, or if there is strife and lack of peace in any area right now, rest assured. In our natural flesh, we are weak and easily troubled by what we see around us. Maybe your child is rebellious, or mixing with the wrong company, there is a lack of funds, or sickness in the family. The Holy Spirit is leading you to turn your eyes to Jesus.

He wants you first to come and enjoy His fellowship and companionship. To bask in His presence and enjoy His peace and loveliness. Start to see Him in your home. See His love, grace, blessing, and provision over your family and finances, and rest in Him. Will you yield to His leading? In due time, His divine, perfect peace and joy will lift you above the challenges, and you start to see His blessings unfold.

Look to Jesus, behold His wonderful face, and bask in His presence, peace, calm, and love. Take time to thank Him and praise Him for all His goodness, faithfulness and love. Meditate on scriptures of His promises for you. Dwell more and more with Jesus and as you do so, you soon come into God's blessings with joy, peace and contentment. Amen.

Day 95—Your Blessings Are Guaranteed by the Lord

> The Lord will guarantee a blessing on everything you do and will fill your storehouses with grain. The Lord your God will bless you in the land he is giving you. (Deuteronomy 28:8 NLT)

God's blessings are guaranteed for you. He makes sure you have more than enough to meet all your needs because He cares for you. He will bless you wherever He places you— your home, workplace, or ministry. You may ask why you still have those debts, why the business is slow, and why there's still no peace at home. Do not be anxious. The Lord is true, and His promises are good.

I remember when I was working and getting a good income. At the time, life for me was about earning and saving for retirement, but nothing felt enough no matter how much I had in the bank. Like many in the world, I was fearful and insecure, always feeling like I didn't have enough for the future. Nothing was guaranteed.

But when I encountered Jesus and His love, my life was transformed. My hope and joy turned to Christ, and my thoughts were directed to Him and all that He did for me at the cross. When I believed His abundant provision and embraced a lifestyle of surrendering to Him instead of to my flesh, I came into such wonderful blessing that were beyond my imagination. He lifted me from being insecure about my future to enjoying a sense of eternity. For nine years I have not worked for an income, yet He always provided abundantly. He brought me a wonderful husband and an instant family. He opened up areas of ministry for us that brought such satisfaction—all because of trusting and completely yielding to Him.

Yield to and rest in Jesus. His blessings for you are guaranteed, and when you draw close to Him, spend time enjoying His presence, and trust Him in everything, you will see His blessings flow to you and your family, because God desires to bless you. Amen.

Day 96—Sin in a Believer's Life

> We know that God's children do not make a practice of sinning, for God's Son holds them securely, and the evil one cannot touch them. (1 John 5:18 NLT)

> But the hour is coming, and now is, when the true worshipers will worship the Father in spirit and truth; for the Father is seeking such to worship Him. (John 4:23 NKJ)

As a new creation in Christ, our spirit has been sanctified and the life and light of the Holy Spirit in us draws us towards God and causes us to lose the desire to sin. But we still have the weak, un-renewed soul and body (our flesh) that leads us to make mistakes and fall into sin. When that happens, we know we are out of line with God's ways and we feel uneasy because our spirit is uncomfortable with sin. Having a tender conscience, we may even mistake our discomfort with our flesh sin as God being upset and unhappy with us. All sin does is make us remorseful, sorry and ashamed. Does this speak to you?

This is where the Holy Spirit wants to remind you that there is no condemnation in Christ Jesus. He will always love you, bless, protect, lift, honour and satisfy you. He continues to see you as perfect and holy. You are secure in God's hand for all eternity. God does not forsake us, or stop loving us because of the sins of our flesh. This is where we can ask His help, for His Spirit to strengthen us. And He is ready to lift and strengthen us to walk more righteously.

However, some think that because Christ has forgiven our sins, therefore, sin does not exist anymore. Others think that since our sins are forgiven and there is no condemnation in Christ, they can sin freely without consequences. Others have redefined sin to suit their life choices and decisions or those of their loved ones. They quench the prodding of the Holy Spirit and numb any discomfort towards sin.

When a believer deliberately sins, and numbs his conscience, he is taking the sacrifice of Jesus lightly. Jesus paid the punishment for sin to set us free from it, not for us to continue to indulge in it and incur the consequences of sin, which eventually leads to death.

A believer who deliberately sins is dominated by rational thinking and emotions (the soul, the flesh), not by the Spirit. When he rationalises that there is no such thing as sin, or he redefines sin to suit his life choices, he rationalises as the world does. He is no longer walking with the counsel of the Holy Spirit, because the Holy Spirit will always lead in true meekness, humility, and submission to the truth of God, not to human emotions, feelings, or reasoning.

Worshipping God in spirit and in truth is a delightful place of fellowship with Him. He leads us on a path of His righteousness paved with peace, joy, satisfaction, and fulfilment. When we deliberately stay in sin, or redefine sin to suit our life choices, we are ruled by rational thinking and emotions (our soul and our flesh), and have moved from worshiping him in spirit and in truth. We have moved outside of His true fellowship.

The good news is that God loves us dearly. He is grieved by our choices, but He is kind, merciful, gracious, forgiving, and ever loving. His arms are stretched out, ready to hug you and bring you into His truth and fellowship. He is ready to restore to you whatever was taken—years that are lost, or relationships that must be cut. He can bring such divine joy, contentment and satisfaction upon your life. The Holy Spirit will never stop reaching out to you to come to repentance (change your mind to align with God's ways) because God desires for you to come into fellowship with Him.

Take time to be renewed by the Word of God and the counsel of the Holy Spirit. Quieten those emotions and that rationalising mind. Seek the Word and the Holy Spirit. Allow Him to show you and flood you with His truth, love, and light; to lead you to repentance which is simply changing your mind and aligning with God's truths and ways. He longs for your fellowship and for you to come to Him. He has a much more wonderful path ahead for you.

Day 97—Do Not Be Tired of Doing Good

> But those who live to please the Spirit will harvest everlasting life from the Spirit. So let's not get tired of doing what is good. At just the right time we will reap a harvest of blessing if we don't give up. (Galatians 6:8b–9 NLT)

In the spirit we are made perfect, but our flesh and body have not been perfected. They are undergoing sanctification as we renew our minds by the Word of God. In our flesh is a tendency to sin and do its own thing apart from the truth of God.

It's a battle that all believers go through. God's Spirit in you compels you to demonstrate His character, love, joy, patience, kindness, goodness, mercy, faithfulness, and self-control so the world can see His love and come to Him. But the lazy flesh ignores the Spirit's promptings and chooses to stay impatient, unkind, arrogant, unloving, ungracious, and unfaithful, lacking self-control.

Paul tells us to please the Spirit because in doing so, we reap a harvest of everlasting life! Imagine all the souls that are impacted for Christ simply because you choose to please the Spirit and not your flesh. The Spirit prompts you to reach out to someone, give an encouraging word, visit someone or pray for someone. He prompts you to refrain from gossiping, saying hurtful things. Have you experienced the joy and satisfaction when you do as prompted by the Spirit?

Yield to the Holy Spirit, who always leads you in God's light, truth and wisdom. He leads you to love others, to be gracious, but also to speak His truth. Take time, quieten your mind, and listen to the Holy Spirit's gentle leading on the inside. Yield to the Holy Spirit, one incident at a time and soon your flesh will line up with the Spirit. Living for God's sake becomes second nature and His love, joy, peace, satisfaction, fulfilment, increases for you.

Day 98—Jesus Gave You His Name and Authority

> Therefore God also has highly exalted Him and given Him
> the name which is above every name, that at the name of
> Jesus every knee should bow…. (Philippians 2:9–10a NKJV)

God has exalted Jesus and given Him the name that is above all names. His name is above the name of any sickness, lack, every evil, rebellion and sin. At His name, every knee will bow; the devil has to bow, let go, and leave; sicknesses, lack, oppression, and all troubles have to bow and leave.

When you believe Jesus, His name is given to you. You are called a Christian. On top of that, He also gives you His authority. When you exercise the authority that He gives you, the devil has to bow to you just like he has to bow to Jesus. You have His ability to walk thriving in His shalom peace in the face of trials and things that come against you.

See yourself having His authority. Believe with your heart and keep His name close to your lips. Align your thoughts and your speech with His thoughts towards you. Exercise your authority and declare what God has for you and your family, even if you are not seeing it yet. Be very bold and decree in the name of Jesus, and see things change in your life.

Declare, "My children shall live out all the plans and purposes that God has for them". In the midst of struggling with your weaknesses, declare, 'I am weak but in Him, I am strong". In struggling with anger issues, declare, "I am the righteousness of God in Christ and I shall grow in love, kindness and gentleness towards people". When symptoms come against you, declare, "Jesus's body was striped for my healing. I receive my healing, Thank You Lord. Amen".

Continue to decree with boldness who you are in Christ, and declare according to God's thoughts, His protection, provision and blessings for you and your loved ones.

Day 99—The Lord Hears When You, the Righteous One, Cries Out

> The righteous cry out, and the LORD hears, And delivers them out of all their troubles. (Psalm 34:17)

You are priceless to our heavenly Father. He did not redeem you with what is perishable; He redeemed you with the precious, divine, eternal blood of Jesus so that your salvation is eternal. You are righteous in Christ.

Our mistakes and failures, and the consequences (pain and suffering) that come with these mistakes, may cause us to have doubts about our position with God. We have all been there. I met a young lady who got into wrong company and ended up living a promiscuous life. After a few years, she became depressed, ashamed, and filled with guilt and condemnation. She felt worthless and thought that God had written her off. Even after she became a believer, she continued struggling with sin, condemnation, and her past. Do you know someone who still struggles in this area?

After having heard countless times about God's love for her, she finally received revelation of Jesus's precious sacrifice for her. She was indeed forgiven and there was no more condemnation. Her life turned around. The shame and depression lifted; the nightmares stopped. She continued to grow with Jesus, walking in His truths, and began to glow with a peace, calm and joy. Today she is happily married with a beautiful family and is serving God.

Surely the Lord hears and delivers you out of your troubles when you keep coming to Him for help. Do not give up, do not stop coming to Him. Even though the situation may seem unchanged, something in the supernatural happens when you come to Jesus. In due time, you will receive revelation that sets you free.

> Thank You, Lord Jesus that in You, my salvation is secure. Help me, Lord, to walk in the freedom this redemption has given me—freedom from sin, freedom from destructive habits—so that I may live gloriously for You. Teach me to grow in greater knowledge and understanding of Your love and grace. Amen.

Day 100—His Grace Increases More Where Sin Is Greatest

> Moreover the law entered that the offense might abound. But where sin abounded, grace abounded much more. (Romans 5:20 NKJV)

God has no desire to see any of us missing the glorious plans that He has for us. He does not desire to see anyone living in anger, hatred, fear, anxiety, lack, depression, or unsatisfied.

God is not waiting to punish us when we fail or fall into sin. Instead, He gently corrects us, pours out more love and grace, and waits with open arms to welcome us back. It grieves Him that we turn away from Him because of our sin, shame and guilt. It pains Him to see us totally blinded and consumed by sin. When we come humbly to Him, desiring to change our ways, His power is there to lift us from sin to a more righteous life.

Are you living in guilt, condemnation, and shame because of your past? Are you not able to move past your mistakes and failures? God is pouring more love and grace upon you because He desires to see you come to the fullness of His love and forgiveness for you.

Take heart when you miss it, or when you see sin in the lives of those you love and in the world around us. Know that where sin is great, God's love and grace is even bigger and stronger because God does not desire that anyone goes without His grace and love.

> Thank You, Jesus, for Your wonderful love for me. Give me more revelation that Your love and grace increases for me when I fall into sin and that You do not stop loving me just because I miss it. I open my heart to receive this truth. Help me to walk in the fullness of this, trusting You and being transformed by the power of Your love and grace to live more righteously and free of sin. Amen.

Day 101—Come Boldly to God the Father for Mercy

> Let us therefore come boldly to the throne of grace, that we may obtain mercy and find grace to help in time of need. (Hebrews 4:16 NKJV)

As believers, there will be times when our flesh gets the better of us and we fail, fall into sin, and feel shame and guilt. Does this speak to you? We all have been there, and God knows our weakness. He knows our human minds. He knows that the enemy is capable of condemning us. That's why He gave us this scripture to assure us that we are deeply loved; and can always come boldly to Him. You are loved and accepted by God not because you are wonderful, spotless and faultless, but because Christ is wonderful and sinless and you are in Him.

As a young believer, I had to keep reminding myself that I was in Christ and that God loved me. He was not counting my sins and mistakes against me and that I could go boldly to Him. If you likewise feel shame and guilt when you fail, remember that your heavenly Father dwells on a throne not of judgment but of His grace and love. His grace and His unending, unconditional love is there regardless of what you may have done. He is always extending His love, help, and comfort to you. Jesus's finished work at the cross secured that for us.

God is waiting for you with love and grace to empower you and lift you above those weaknesses and temptations. 'But my problems are so huge. I have been stuck with this weakness for years,' you may argue. Well, our God is much bigger than any problem and any challenge.

On your own, you cannot. But when you come to Him, He is able to lift you above any failure, weakness and temptation. Come boldly to Him. He is waiting with open arms, ready to receive you, hug you, pour His grace and mercy on you, and restore you to walk in righteousness, peace and joy.

Take time to praise and thank Jesus for all that He has done for you.

Day 102—Jesus Is Now Interceding for You

> Who is he who condemns? It is Christ who died, and furthermore is also risen, who is even at the right hand of God, who also makes intercession for us. (Romans 8:34 NKJV)

As we continue in our faith, we will at times succumb to weaknesses and fail to overcome bad habits; this could cause us to condemn ourselves. Well-meaning people point out our shortcomings or tell us we're not behaving as Christians. Often the enemy throws thoughts at us that lead to condemnation, telling us how terrible we are, how we have messed up, how we are not good enough, or how we don't measure up.

Don't receive these accusations. The truth is that God finds you totally acceptable in Christ. Your spirit is completely righteous in His sight. God is not finding fault with you or your behaviour, and He wants you to know that. He wants you to know all that Jesus has gone through to bring righteousness to you, and that Jesus is today still making intercession for you.

He desires for our minds and emotions, our flesh, to be brought into alignment with His nature. Jesus is still working and interceding for us so that we keep growing, believing, and coming to Him. We will keep looking to Him because looking to Him is how we become transformed to be like Him.

Do not be discouraged when you or others fail as believers. You are dearly loved and precious to Him. Continue to see yourself as the righteousness of God in Christ. Jesus redeemed you two thousand years ago, and He continues to work for you, interceding for you today. As you look to Him, surrender and yield to Him, He is able to supernaturally deliver you out of your failures and weaknesses.

Take time and thank and praise Jesus for all that He continues to do for you.

Day 103—God's Ways Are Higher Than Our Ways

> As the heavens are higher than the earth, So are my ways higher than your ways, and my thoughts than your thoughts. (Isaiah 55:9 NKJV)

Man is proud and arrogant, thinking highly of himself. His ways are strife, cunning and deceit to get ahead. Others see no value in themselves. They feel like failures, they feel condemned, fearful, depressed, worthless, and hopeless. Man's ways, whether full of pride or lacking self-worth, are wrought with pain, destructive thinking and habits, disappointment, bondages, and sorrows.

The good news is that Jesus came and dealt with all the lowly ways of the world at the cross. He came to bring us eternity and God's higher ways which are love, peace, joy, hope, blessings, flourishing in our ways, and freedom from condemnation, pride and self-glory. His finished work at the cross sets us free to enter the higher ways of God!

You ask, "How do I live in the higher ways of God?" He beckons you to come to Him, into His presence, and in His Word. Be humble and allow the Holy Spirit His place in your heart. As you do so, you start to let go of pride, arrogance and stubbornness. You start letting go of anxieties, condemnation, and feelings of worthlessness. The Holy Spirit takes over and lifts you. He cleanses you and fills you with our Father's love for you. He shows you that you are His beloved child and you have an eternal home with Him. He fills you with His bountiful fruits; His love, joy, peace, favour, goodness, hope, protection, every good thing.

So today, would you commit to abide in Jesus? Would you let the Holy Spirit reign freely in your life? And yield and submit to His promptings? He is there to lift you above the mundane and the mediocre to His higher ways of love, kindness, goodness, patience, peace, joy, thriving, all possibilities, fulfilment, and satisfaction for His glory.

Day 104—Meditate in Your Heart and Be Still

> Be angry, and do not sin. Meditate within your heart on your
> bed, and be still. (Psalm 4:4 NKJV)

God's Spirit is communicating with us all the time, but quite often in the busyness of the day and all the tasks that need to be done, we face the loudness of our own thoughts, fears, and worries. While trying to solve problems using our smarts, we fail to hear His still, small voice whispering His thoughts and heart towards us.

In His wisdom, God tells us to be still. Be at rest. Restrain from using that phone to grumble and complain to someone. Quieten that active mind with the hundreds of thoughts racing around. Start listening inward, where His Spirit dwells.

Be quiet, be still, and hear His Spirit. Know that He is God who speaks to you, breathing His peace, calm, rest, and joy. He always speaks peace to you. He speaks healing and reassurance. He speaks comfort and encouragement. He leads you to rest and not worry and fret. His voice will calm you and not push or rush you. His voice restores you and calms your fears and confusion.

His voice brings joy into your heart and dispels condemnation. He speaks conviction in your heart to love, forgive and let go of anger. In the midst of feeling confused, pushed, rushed, fearful, discouraged, worried, unforgiving, angry, or condemned, come and be still and hear God's voice. Be set free to enter into His love, peace, joy, comfort, and encouragement.

As you rest in Him, you start to align your life and decisions with God's best for you. You begin to enjoy a divine tranquility from within. In that place, when we are quietened and filled with His love, peace, and joy, in the presence of all the external circumstances, that is when God is exalted, and His glory shines in our lives.

Praise Jesus for His wondrous finished work that has made all this possible.

Day 105—He Made Everything Beautiful

> He made everything beautiful in its time. (Ecclesiastes 3:11a
> NKJV)

God made everything beautiful and good: the mountains, hills, and plains with all their flora and fauna, as well as the rivers and seas. You and I are the crowning glory of His creation, and we are meant to live the beautiful life in Christ that He has prepared for us. But how could He have created everything beautiful when there is so much suffering, pain, and troubles in this world?

Because of Adam, the world is fallen and under the dominion of Satan, the one that steals, kills, and destroys. The devil continues to fabricate disasters, symptoms, and wrong thinking to instil fear, anxiety, anger, and all kinds of negative feelings. He gives suggestions to keep people in bondage to destructive habits, and he creates lies to blind the world from the truths of God.

Christ came to redeem fallen people and restore the dominion back to them. When you come to Christ, you received His life and the devil loses his power to defeat or destroy you. God is there for us and when we let Him, He will turn things around for us so that we come into a place of greater love, peace, joy, trust, rest, and blessing.

When we come to Christ, we become His body here on earth. We are tasked to share His love, truth, and salvation with the rest of the world. God desires for His salvation to reach all man, and for all to come into His kingdom and take back the dominion from the devil. Then the devil's work to destroy, steal, and kill has to come to an end. All sufferings and problems lose their power and come to an end, and all things become restored to beautiful in Christ again.

Because you are in Christ, the devil has lost his dominion over you. Therefore continue to stay rooted in Him, grow strong in Him and in the knowledge of His love. Go on and share His love with others, pray with them, bring His light to them and see His love, grace, and beauty restored in others' lives. What joy for you when that happens!

Day 106—In Christ, You Enter into God's Rest

For we who have believed do enter that rest. (Hebrews 4:3a NKJV)

The world is not at rest. We see terror and violence unleashed in the most shocking way. We see natural disasters that destroy whole cities. We see suffering and lack. There's stress making a living to provide for the family. People are anxious about their children, their health. The world finds ways and means to cope with life.

But in Christ, you are set free and have entered a place of His peace and rest. In Him, we are protected from all harm and evil. In Him, we have access to the resources of heaven and His ability and solutions to overcome and be victorious. In Christ, we can truly rest from worries and fears; we can rest from striving and struggling on our own because His supernatural abilities are at work for us.

You may ask, 'How do I rest when I am troubled, anxious, fearful, helpless, and hopeless? When I'm overwhelmed by what I see and by all the circumstances?' Instead of spending time dwelling on the circumstances and problems, take time to appreciate Jesus for everything that He has done for you.

Read God's Word, meditate on it, be still and listen. His Spirit in you is always there to bring you His light, thoughts, ideas, peace, joy, and refreshment. The great I Am dwells within you—He is your peace, joy, hope and way maker. Each time you are tempted to worry, turn your eyes to Jesus. Think of something He has done for you and thank Him. Your mind cannot dwell on Jesus and His wonderful love, peace, and joy while at the same time remain worrisome. Those worrisome thoughts have to go in His presence!

See Him in your present situation. See His love, ability, and power in your situation. As you do so, you begin to rest in Him. Spend that sweet time with Him, and let His love, peace, joy, ideas and thoughts overwhelm you and fill you.

Day 107—How Come There Are Still Calamities and Problems?

> Just as I swore in the time of Noah that I would never again
> let a flood cover the earth, so now I swear that I will never
> again be angry and punish you. (Isaiah 54:9 NKJV)

If God swore that He would never be angry or punish us again, then why do we still see so much suffering, sickness, and calamity in the world? Why do we see so many innocent people suffering without basic necessities?

Firstly, God does not bring sufferings, calamities, and sicknesses. These resulted from Adam's disobedience, which brought on death and also curses. His dominion over the world was also handed to Satan. So Satan has a right to bring on disasters and influence the minds of people to destruction because the world is under his dominion. Satan's agenda is to steal, kill, and destroy.

But fear not. God has already given us Jesus, who took the punishment of Adam's sin upon Himself. He has set us free from Satan's dominion, death, fear and curses. He has defeated the devil on our behalf. In Him, the devil has no more dominion, no more power over us. In Christ, we can stand victorious in this fallen world. The world continues in decay, calamities, negative and destructive thinking, but in Him we have divine protection, abundance of His love, peace, joy, blessings and well-being for eternity. God desires that the world comes to Christ and be set free from Satan's dominion.

When symptoms, challenges, and accidents come against you, know that these are the consequences of your choices, and the natural effects of the fallen world. It is not God punishing you or teaching you a lesson. He loves you. He sent His Son Jesus to set you free from the devil's dominion, and the effects of the fallen world. Today, you enjoy His divine protection.

In times of trials, turn your eyes to God, align yourself with Him, quiet down, and come humbly to Him for help and guidance so that you walk in alignment with His ways and plans for you, which are of peace, joy, gladness of heart, and protection in the face of calamities.

Day 108—The Lord Your God Rejoices over You

> The Lord your God in your midst, the Mighty One, will save; He will rejoice over you with gladness, He will quiet *you* with His love, He will rejoice over you with singing. (Zephaniah 3:17 NKJV)

When we look at all that is happening in the world, the values that prevail, the economic uncertainty, the natural calamities, it may dismay us, and we wonder where God is. Sometimes the trials, problems, and challenges seem so unrelenting, and our hearts are filled with fear and dread. However, as believers, it is important for us to know the truth. It is the enemy of God at work in this world, and he targets God's children to discourage them, to cast doubts, and hijack them from the truth. He is out to create troubles, bring on disasters, and mess with people's thinking. His agenda is to steal, kill, and destroy.

But child of God, you have nothing to fear because the Lord God is in your midst. He is watching over you, protecting you and keeping you safe. What you need to do to guard your heart against the works of the enemy is to know how great and awesome your heavenly Father is. And to know the extent of His love for you.

Your heavenly Father loves you dearly. You are special and precious to Him. He takes much pleasure and delight in you. You make Him smile with gladness and He is rejoicing over you with singing. He longs more than anything to quiet your fears and anxieties with His love.

Therefore quieten your heart and those raging thoughts. Be still and invite the Holy Spirit to fill you with His love and peace. Look up to Jesus and be filled with the love, gladness, and rejoicing of your heavenly Father. Spend time in God's word, in His presence, reminding yourself constantly of His love, goodness, thoughts, and heart towards you. As your heart and mind refocus back on the Lord Jesus and as you see His love and His heart towards you, you realise that indeed God is in your midst. He has never left you or forsaken you. His gentle, calm, peaceable, quiet love and strength will lift you. Come to Him always.

Day 109—No Weapon Formed against You Shall Prosper

> No weapon formed against you shall prosper, and every tongue which rises against you in judgment You shall condemn. This is the heritage of the servants of the Lord, and their righteousness is from Me. (Isaiah 54:17 NJKV)

This scripture tells us that no weapons formed against us can prosper. It doesn't matter what the enemy plots. He will throw negative thoughts at us, defeating thoughts, condemnation, fears, worries, and anxiety. People may speak lies and accusations against us. The enemy uses all these weapons to try to defeat us, to steal the love, peace and joy that is ours in Christ. But because we are His righteous ones, the Lord Himself will ensure that these weapons of the enemy cannot succeed against us.

Do the obstacles, problems, and challenges confronting you seem unbearable? Are there people who are always working against you? Is there someone grumbling about you, gossiping about you, or back-stabbing you? Know the truth and don't allow these to steal your peace and joy and victory.

You are God's beloved, righteous child and He is on your side, fighting for you. When God is on your side, nothing can come against you. God is for you. His protection and favour is on you, and He is your defence. Nothing that the devil or man plan against you will succeed. What the enemy throws at you will fall to the ground and come to nothing! Therefore, do not lose heart when everything seems to be against you, because when you have Jesus as your Lord and Master, He fights your battles for you.

Instead, rejoice in the midst of your trials. Look to Jesus and rejoice that you have such a wonderful Saviour and Master. Keep your gaze on Him, the One who has redeemed you. He will cause things to turn around for you. Those weapons of the enemy will soon self-destruct and fall to nothing, while you continue to grow in the grace and love of Jesus.

Day 110—The Lord Is Your Shield

> But You, O LORD, are a shield for me, My glory and the
> One who lifts up my head. (Psalm 3:3 NJKV)

A shield is a defence that soldiers use during battles. It is used to protect the soldier against offensive arrows and spears of the enemy. Today, there is an enemy of God who is out to attack us because he is upset that Jesus has defeated him and that through Jesus, we have been given eternal life, with heaven's resources made available to us.

He is already defeated, yet he sneaks around shooting fiery arrows of lies, doubts, fears, and temptations to trip us and blind us to God's love, provision, and blessings. He cannot take from us the eternal redemption that is ours in Christ, or our access to the kingdom of heaven, but he will do all he can to steal our peace and joy and disrupt the wonderful plans that God has for us here on earth. He does all he can with lying thoughts and temptations to stop us from living the overcoming life that speaks of the love of Jesus. He is so angry with what God has given to us through Jesus.

But you have no fear of him because Jesus is your shield. You ask, 'How does Jesus become my shield?' Come to Him often. Read the Word and know Him, know how much He loves you. Rest in His presence, and see His peace, joy, patience, kindness, compassion and strength. See the enemy cowering in His light. Know that he is already defeated and is merely waiting his final judgement. When tempting, lying, and fearful thoughts hit you, and when trials come against you or your loved ones, know that these are simply desperate measures by the enemy to steal your peace and joy. But he can't hurt you because Jesus is your shield.

Put Jesus first in every situation and decision. Let Him be there in all your moments, thanking Him, blessing and honouring Him. Stay close to Jesus, and allow Him to protect and guard your heart and mind. When He is your shield, those fiery darts and arrows of the enemy will come to nothing and you stand triumph, in His joy and peace.

Day 111—The Weapons of Our Warfare Are Mighty in God

> For the weapons of our warfare are not carnal but mighty in God for pulling down strongholds, casting down arguments and every high thing that exalts itself against the knowledge of God, bringing every thought into captivity to the obedience of Christ. (2 Corinthians 10:4–5 NKJV)

The greatest threats that we face today are the thoughts, reasoning, and arguments that come against God's love and truth. You entertain thoughts that you are worthless and unlovable. You allow fearful and anxious thoughts about your health, finances or future to weaken you. You dwell so much on problems that you feel depressed and hopeless. This is the enemy's way to make you feel defeated and take you further away from the abundance that God has for your life.

What can you do to defend yourself? The weapons of this warfare are not by carnal, human ways of reasoning, analysing away the problems. Neither is it by drinking, drugging, or medicating to numb the pain and fears. The weapons of our warfare are found in Christ alone.

In the face of all the thoughts that we are assailed with, keep looking to Jesus and what He has done for you. You are a new creation in Him. You have His life. You are dearly loved, a beloved child of the Most High God. You are the apple of His eye. He desires to put His arms around you, comfort you, and fill you with His love, joy, and peace. He wants to ease away all the pain, sadness, and fear. Will you let Him?

Come to Jesus. See His wondrous finished work at the cross. Come with an open heart and receive the love that God has for you. Soon you find that the strongholds and wrong thoughts can't condemn you. You have the strength to not act on them. They are gone, and you are set free to love and worship God. Your life becomes filled with His love, peace, joy, and possibilities. Keep so close to Him, and all those wrong thoughts and strongholds have to give way to Him. Look to Jesus now and say, 'Lord, fill my heart and mind with Your love, peace, joy, life, grace and truth. Give me more revelation so that I can walk in Your victory. Amen.'

Day 112—You Will Reflect God's Glory

> Arise, shine; For your light has come. And the glory of the
> LORD is risen upon you. For behold, the darkness shall cover
> the earth, And deep darkness the people; But the LORD will
> arise over you, And His glory will be seen upon you. (Isaiah
> 60:1–2 NKJV)

What an honour and blessing that we get to live in the time that Isaiah 60 prophesised about. The glory of God is on us because Christ, the Light of the world, has come and has given us His light.

Today, we see so much darkness in the world around us. We see the teachings of God being ridiculed. What is evil is called good, and what is good is called evil. We see all kinds of destruction and terror, which stem from the deep darkness of the fallen human heart. We also see climactic calamities—earthquakes, volcanoes, hurricanes, and destructive storms on a scale and frequency not witnessed before.

But we shall have no fear because His light is upon us and His Spirit lives in us. His eternal joy, peace, and wisdom are ours because we are His beloved people. We will go out in His love, mercy, grace, peace, joy, and hope, becoming His light to a world that is in darkness. We are neither dismayed nor discouraged by the darkness around us. Instead, we have His power to rise up and reflect His glory.

Always remember that you are in this world but not of this world. You are His beloved child. His Spirit lives in you, and He is with you at all times. You are a citizen of heaven and you have a right to the resources of heaven. Peace, joy, healing, favor, protection, wisdom, strength are yours. When you see darkness, have no fear; your help comes from God, who is the creator of heaven and earth. His resources and abilities are available to you. His light is risen upon you. And surely, as you walk in His light, the people around you see His light. And are drawn to the glory of the Saviour and Lover of our souls. Hallelujah!

Day 113—He Will Grant the Desires of Your Heart

> Delight yourself in the Lord, And He will give you the desires of your heart. (Psalm 37:4 NKJV)

Have you ever pursued all kinds of pleasures and entertainment but still feel empty inside? Most of us can relate to this. Because deep within each of us is a longing for the divine. Jesus, the perfect Son of God is the only One who can satisfy that deep longing in us. He is the true desire of our hearts. When we find our delight in Him, He will grant our heart's desires.

We delight in the Lord by reading God's Word, feeding on Him, seeing His majesty, humility, love and compassion for all mankind. You look to Him to find purpose in your life. You allow Him to lead and guide you to become established in His love, peace, and joy. As you are reading this and meditating on Him, you are delighting in Him and that pleases Him!

When you feel like the Lord is not granting your heart's desire, you might check first where and how you are finding delight for your life. Are you hankering after things in the world, or are you delighting in Him, finding your joy and purpose in Him?

When you delight in Him, you see Him more clearly in the full revelation of His love, grace, majesty and perfection. As you keep seeing Him in His full splendour, you become transformed to be like Him: at peace, at rest, joyful, and overflowing with divine confidence and strength. In that place of fellowship and intimacy with Him, delighting in Him, you find your desires become transformed and what is important to Him becomes important to you. He fills you with satisfaction and divine purpose.

Come to Him often. Find your delight in Him. Doing so brings you into the divine life and purpose of God. When you delight in Him and your desires are aligned to His, He will never disappoint you, nor leave you unsatisfied and unfulfilled!

Day 114—He Is the Only Way to the Father

'I am the way, the truth and the life. No one comes to the
Father except through Me.' (John 14:6 NKJV)

Religions are man's efforts to win God's forgiveness, approval and blessings
and to avert punishment. At the core of every religion is a basic teaching about
living a good and moral life. It often comes with a list of rules to follow in
order to be blessed and rituals to carry out to ward off evil. Religions come
in many names and are man's attempts to give himself a sense of connection
with the divine and to transcend the challenges of this life.

The prevailing idea in the world is that all religions are the same; they all lead
to God. Have you ever heard or been told that? Perhaps you yourself used to
think that.

Our God Himself, Creator, holy and majestic, provided a way for us to
connect with Him. Jesus is God's own way for us to come into relationship
with Him. Jesus came not with a set of rules, of dos and don'ts, or rituals
to gain God's acceptance. Instead of demanding sacrifices from us for our
sins, Jesus came and died on the cross, forgave us our sins, and set us free
from condemnation. He came and took care of the most basic problem that
man faces, that of sin and condemnation. And He gave us His Spirit and life
that we might live in eternal relationship with our heavenly Father. The only
condition is that we believe He is the Way to God, the Truth and the Life.

He is the only way into eternity with God. God's way is not about a set of rules
and rituals or living a good and moral life. It is about being in relationship
with God the Father through Jesus His Son who purified and qualified us to
come into God's holy presence.

Jesus alone provides the way for you to enter into the life that only God the
Father can give: a life of love, joy, peace, possibilities, provision, protection,
blessings and hope. It's about a new identity as a new creation, a dearly beloved
child of God Most High, a citizen of heaven, a life in relationship with Him
for eternity.

Day 115—Not Only You but Your Household Shall Be Saved

> So they said, 'Believe on the Lord Jesus Christ, and you will be saved, you and your household.' (Acts 16:31 NKJV)

Are there loved ones in your family who do not know Jesus as their Lord and Saviour? Perhaps their lives are messed up. Are there family members who oppose you for believing Jesus? Do not lose heart for God has promised that when you are saved, your household will be saved too.

Stay focussed on your fellowship with Jesus, and as you shine in the abundance of His love, joy, and peace, your light surely cannot go unnoticed by those closest to you. Continue to extend His love towards them and persist to do good to them as Jesus would. As you mirror His love to those around you and pray for them, the Holy Spirit goes to work to convict their hearts.

My own mother resisted the Gospel message until she was ninety years old. We continued to share Jesus's love for her and prayed with her. One day, she just got it. She came to Christ and lived three more glorious, joyful years eagerly reading God's Word daily. She was so confident of her eternal future with Jesus that she told us we should celebrate at her funeral and not wear black (mourning colour). We did so, wearing bright colours at her funeral, to the consternation of those who came to pay their last respects!

Be encouraged. Continue to pray for those you love, and continue to glow in the love, joy, and peace, sharing your blessing with them. Be patient in the Lord and never stop doing these things, and surely you will see lives changed and transformed for the Lord.

> Lord Jesus, I commit _____ [names of those you want to see saved] into Your hands. I pray that You send believers into their lives who will share Your word and love. I ask Lord, that You personally encounter them so that they will see You and know Your love for them. Amen.

Day 116—Jesus Alone Saves

> In Him we have redemption through His blood, the forgiveness of sins, in accordance with the riches of God's grace. (Ephesians 1:7 NKJV)

All of us know of people who, in their pride or stubbornness, refuse to come to God. They think they can save themselves from sins, sicknesses, pains, and sorrows. The truth is we can't save ourselves. Neither can money, gold, the economy, medical experts, or politicians. This is so glaringly true when we look at the world today and the lives of rich and famous personalities who live without God. Sadly their struggles, pains, bondages to substances, relationship problems, and depression are unfairly displayed for the world to see.

Nothing can save us from sin and an eternity dominated by the devil except Jesus, the perfect and innocent Lamb. His divine blood shed for us cleansed us of our sins and made us pure and righteous. His blood gave us new life in Him and defeated death for us. His death, burial and resurrection defeated the devil, setting us free from his dominion.

Jesus bore the stripes and scourges to give us healing. He became our curse to set us free from curses. He was rich but became poor so we can receive the provision of our heavenly Father. He bore our pains and sorrows and in return gave us His love, joy, and peace. The problems, challenges, and struggles of this world cannot ensnare us because we have His resources and authority to overcome.

Continue to pray for your loved ones who are too proud or stubborn to come to God. Pray that their hearts are softened and the scales fall from their eyes. Pray that they see the love of Jesus for them and His redeeming finished work at the cross.

> Lord, I commit _____ to You. I ask that You continue to pursue them with Your love. Encounter them with Your grace and light. Open their spiritual eyes, give them a glimpse of the glorious eternal life of true freedom, peace and joy in You. Amen

Day 117—We Have a Ministry from God

> Now all things are of God, who has reconciled us to Himself through Jesus Christ, and has given us the ministry of reconciliation. (2 Corinthians 5:18 NKJV)

We have a ministry to bring God's love and hope to others. God gives us this ministry not to burden us. Christ lives in us. We have His ability and sharing His love with others becomes our spiritual food. It is life giving, filling us with joy and satisfaction and keeping us rooted to Him. Have you experienced satisfaction when you share His love with others, even when they reject you? How much more joy and gladness when someone's heart opens to Christ, His love and salvation.

There is no one better than you and I who have tasted His love, forgiveness, and goodness to share Him with our family and friends. Who can argue with our testimonies, our experience of being set free from condemnation, bondage, fear, anxieties and coming into a wonderful precious hope in return?

Therefore, even as you grow in Christ, start to pray for family members, friends, and co-workers who do not know Him yet. Pray for their hearts to be open, and pray for encounters with the Lord. Show love and be the love of Christ to them. Pray with them when they have a need. When the opportunity presents, share your testimony of how Jesus's love changed your life or how He healed you. When the Holy Spirit brings people to your heart, pray for them, call and talk to them. He may prompt you to visit someone in hospital or visit a neighbor. He may prompt you to lay hands and bring healing to someone. Be bold and step up.

Do not be afraid, wondering what to say. Look to Jesus, trust Him, and He will give you an abundance of words that bless, heal, encourage, comfort, edify, and bring His joy and peace to others. Be bold because when He prompts you, His power is at work for you. He wants to share His love with others, and when you are available for Him, His power and ability will work for you. And it lifts you to a new level of joy and satisfaction in Him!

Day 118—We Are in Christ to Participate in His Redemption Plan

> For we are His workmanship, created in Christ Jesus for good works, which God prepared beforehand that we should walk in them. (Ephesians 2:10 NKJV)

As believers rooted in Christ, we have been blessed not solely for our own pleasure. We are also filled with God's will and desire to do the work that Jesus would do were He physically here on earth. We are His body, His representatives here on earth. And God has good works; works that has eternal impact, divine satisfaction and fulfilment, that He has prepared for us to do.

Do you have a desire to share His love? Or to reach out to those who do not know Him? Do you have a desire to be more generous and kind towards others as an expression of His love? Or a desire to know His Word in greater depth so that you can teach others? Or a desire to care for His people? This is His Spirit calling you to participate in the works that He has prepared for you.

Often the area that God has called us to influence is our immediate connections. As parents, it's to bring up your children in God's truth and love. As colleagues, it's to be exemplary in your attitudes and work ethics. As you pray and seek out what God has for you, start serving with your local church. Often God plants you in local churches to help you grow for what He has prepared for you. Talk to your leaders who also hear from God and they will be able to help mentor you.

As you serve, remain faithful, and prove yourself trustworthy and dependable. Be equipped with the Word, stay close to Jesus, and continue abiding in Him. Keep coming to Him to be filled with His love and grace. He will open doors for you, give you strength and ability to do the assignments that He has prepared for you. When you do the work that He has for you, it will fill you with such joy, fulfilment, and satisfaction for doing them! How wonderful when you see souls redeemed and restored to Him. Participating in what He has prepared for you becomes spiritual food!

Day 119—You Are Anointed by the Spirit of God

> But you have an anointing from the Holy One, and you
> know all things. (1 John 2:20 NKJV)

The word *anoint* comes from ancient sheep farming practice. Shepherds used to pour oil (anoint) on the sheep's head to protect it from the lice and ticks that try to make their way through the wool and into the sheep's ears, eventually killing the sheep. The pests slip off the oily wool, leaving the sheep unharmed. So anointing with oil originated for the purpose of protecting the sheep.

In biblical times, anointing with oil became a symbol of not just protection but also blessing and empowerment for service. In the Bible, anointing has the same action as smearing with oil. In the Old Testament days, when people were called to serve as kings, priests or prophets, and even as artisans for building the temple, they would be anointed with oil to signify that they were chosen, set apart, blessed, equipped, and empowered to do God's work.

In the New Covenant, to be anointed signifies that we are chosen and set apart for God. When you came to Jesus, the Holy Spirit came and now lives in you. You are anointed! You are sealed with the Holy Spirit, set apart for God, and chosen to do the wonderful works that He has prepared for you. It's the same work as Jesus did: to share the Gospel and set captives free.

This anointing of the Holy Spirit is His presence and ability, already in you, to know all the things of God. It is the power of God to help you live holy and glorious and attain to the fullness of Christ. This same anointing transforms your desires and empowers you to share His love with others in a way that touches them and brings light and truth to them.

Therefore do not be fearful or disqualify yourself from sharing His love with others. Perhaps you feel inadequate and imperfect in your ways. Take comfort: it is not about you. It is all about Jesus and His Spirit in you that has made you perfect and given you the opportunity to participate with Him in His work and ministry. He is capable of working all things out.

Your part is to always come to Jesus, continually receive His love and joy, to remind yourself of all that He has done for you and of who you are because of Him. As you abide in Him, He transforms your desires so that what is important to Him becomes important to you. Abiding in Him, you allow the Holy Spirit to release the anointing that is in you. As you live in the power of His presence and anointing, sharing His love becomes a joyous thing. What a blessing that we, His beloved children, get to participate with Him and share in His joy and satisfaction to see lives transformed for His glory!

> Put your hand to your heart and declare, 'I am anointed! I now have the Holy Spirit living in me; the power of God to live righteous and holy, to share His love, and light to the world. Because I am anointed, I can speak words that bring healing, comfort, peace, encouragement, and restoration. I thank You, Lord Jesus, for Your anointing to do the same work that You did here on earth, bringing the good news of our Father's love for us, bringing your forgiveness, healing and blessings to others. Amen.'

You are anointed!

Day 120—Not Our Own Efforts, but the Holy Spirit's

'Not by might nor by power, but by My Spirit,' Says the Lord of hosts. (Zechariah 4:6b NKJV)

God desires to move among us to bring healing, restoration and blessings to His people. But too often, we get in the way with our intellect, rational thinking, emotions, wrong beliefs and ideas. When we allow the Holy Spirit to have His way, the supernatural power of God is released bringing healing and restoration for loss, pain, hurts, sickness, depression, loneliness, and hopelessness.

Years ago, a friend suffered from postnatal depression. We visited her and for no reason, fell into uncontrollable laughter. This friend joined in and we laughed heartily for half an hour. When we finally stopped, our friend's countenance had lifted. That night, she slept soundly for the first time in months. She was completely set free from postnatal depression. On hindsight, we know that the Holy Spirit took over the session to bring healing to a beloved daughter.

The Holy Spirit's cleansing, healing and restoring power is available to all His children because God loves us and desires to help us. He may prompt you to pray, call someone, take a walk, go shopping or in our case, laugh. He has assignments for us to administer healing, restoration and blessing. His ways may be different from what we are familiar with. Let not pride, fear or lack of knowledge keep you from fully cooperating with Him. When we move as He moves, we can expect supernatural results and joy is multiplied! You have nothing to fear when you stay in the Word, abiding in Jesus.

Lord, I desire to learn more about the Holy Spirit, how He leads and moves. I desire to be open to His ways and to always yield to Him, allowing Him to administer healing, restoration and blessing to those around me. Teach me Your ways Holy Spirit. Help me to be less about me and all about You and to truly submit to You. Teach me to co-operate with You fully and become a vessel to minister in Your power. Amen.

Day 121—Jesus Does More Abundantly Than We Can Ask or Think

> Now to Him who is able to do exceedingly abundantly above all that we ask or think, according to the power that works in us. (Ephesians 3:20)

When we abide in Jesus, walk closely with Him, and yield to Him, He can lead us to accomplish much more without strife, and the result is truly beyond what we can think or imagine.

In 2013, my husband and I ended up relocating to the United States, to an area far from family and friends. We were itinerant preachers, but desired for fellowship in a local church, and were led to one, where we developed kingdom friendships that last till today. We were then introduced to a regular local prayer group where lasting friendships were forged. A longing to pray with women led to meeting a precious lady and a woman's Bible study resulted, where we thrived on friendship and encouraging each other in the Lord. A desire to share Christ with others led to a Facebook daily devotional page; and this book being written.

My husband had the opportunity to become a chaplain intern, ministering in a hospital, something he found much satisfaction doing. He then became pastor of a small church near us. Today, we are back in Asia doing what we love best - travelling to teach in Bible schools, enjoying family and friends, fulfilled and satisfied. Only God could do this, smoothing out the path as we make major life changes and moves. He plants us among Kingdom family and friends wherever we go, bringing satisfaction and fulfilment.

We simply followed the desires that the Lord put in our hearts. When one of us sensed the Holy Spirit prompting us to move in a direction or take an action, we would discuss and pray until we both had agreement and peace. Only then would we take steps to follow through. When it is of the Lord, He opens doors and makes all transition smooth, and He does much better than we ourselves can. Therefore be humble and yield to the Holy Spirit's leading, because truly He is able to do much more exceedingly. He brings life and satisfaction abundantly beyond what you can think or imagine.

Day 122—We Have His Spirit of Love

> Now hope does not disappoint, because the love of God has
> been poured out in our hearts by the Holy Spirit who was
> given to us. (Romans 5:5 NKJV)

We all have challenging people in our lives—people who are difficult, who give us headaches and unnecessary troubles, and who make our lives miserable. They could be our spouses, children, siblings, relatives, friends, or co-workers. It is easy to get angry and impatient and write them off.

But through Jesus, God's Spirit of love now dwells in us. He has given us His love so we can thrive and flourish and love others too. Instead of focussing on the person or the problem and getting more upset and disheartened, start to see all that Jesus has done for you. See His love, compassion, and grace. Allow His Spirit of love and compassion to dominate you. Instead of being impatient and angry, His love causes you to understand where others are at and moves you to bless them, to reach out and edify and help them.

I remember an occasion when I was at loggerheads with someone close. I would get angry each time I think of the person. But as I reflected on Jesus's love for me, how He loved me, and how He'd died for me, my heart began to change. I let go of those angry thoughts of the person and began to bless the person and reach out in kindness instead. After months, I saw the person change to become more giving and less selfish.

God's love has been deposited in our heart, enabling us to love everyone. When you dwell in Christ, His Spirit of love begins to dominate you. Dwelling and abiding in Him activates His love in you and it becomes easier for you to let go of your feelings and rights. Instead you allow His love to reign and flow out of you. His Spirit of love deposited in you has moved you to be a witness of His love, grace and light. And in turn others are touched for His glory! Stay blessed, keep abiding in Jesus and let His love reign in you.

Day 123—Love Your Enemies, Do Good to Them, and Bless Them

> But I say to you who hear: Love your enemies, do good to those who hate you, bless those who curse you, and pray for those who spitefully use you. (Luke 6:27–28 NJKV)

As you walk the walk of faith and in the calling that God has for you, you may encounter situations not different from the world. You may feel let down by those you work with, feel betrayed, or have accusations levelled against you. You may be doing as God leads you to do, and yet you have a superior come strongly against you.

When you encounter such situations, know that God is preparing you to mature even more in His love, grace, and forgiveness. First come to the Lord and receive His love for you. His opinion of you matters more than man's. He knows your heart, values and esteems you, and counts you worthy. When you receive Jesus's love, it activates God's love, which has been deposited in your heart. It becomes easy to forgive, do good to those who hurt you, bless them, and pray for them. In doing so, you keep yourself from becoming bitter. You are resting in Christ and letting Him handle the injustice and wrongdoing on your behalf, and He is much more able than you.

The few times when we found ourselves in situations where we felt we were not treated right, we would take a stand not to talk about it with others. Instead, we would forgive, pray, and bless the person. Doing that stopped the situation from escalating, and we drew closer to God, trusting Him to right the situation for us. Over time, we enjoy a greater blessing of His peace and joy knowing He is pleased with us, more open doors, and restoration and reconciliation.

Therefore when someone wrongs you, let self-control dominate. Do not retaliate, get all angry, and bad-mouth the person. Instead, forgive, do good to the person, and bless and pray for the person. Doing that sets you up to enjoy a far greater blessing from God.

Day 124—The Lord Will Guide You Continually

> The LORD will guide you continually, giving you water when you are dry and restoring your strength. You will be like a well-watered garden, like an ever-flowing spring. (Isaiah 58:11 NLT)

As we walk the walk of faith, there may be times that we fall into feeling lonely, heavy-hearted, and powerless. The best of ministers, pastors, Bible teachers, and servers of God can get into this situation, feeling discouraged and powerless. Are you spiritually dry? Are you discouraged, needing refreshment? Do not be disheartened.

The Holy Spirit dwells in you. His anointing is in you. The power of God, the ability of God, and the peace, joy, and refreshing that God has given to all His children who are in Christ Jesus dwells in you. He guides you continually, bringing fresh thoughts and ideas when you run dry. He restores your strength when you are weary and tired so that you are like an ever-flowing spring, always flowing with life. His Spirit working in you causes you to become like a well-watered garden: beautiful, flourishing, and delightful to behold.

When you rest and meditate on Jesus, you release your worries and are able to receive the Holy Spirit's refreshing. Are you weary and lonely? Turn your eyes and heart back to Jesus! Rest your thoughts and mind, and meditate on Him, on His loveliness, and on His great love for you. Soon His sweet fellowship, by the power of the Holy Spirit, will uplift, refresh, and energise you.

While writing this book, there were days when I felt dry, and discouraged, when family issues were overwhelming, and I questioned if I really had anything worth sharing. When that happens, I would come to the Lord, feed on Him, rest in Him. Then I see that it's not about me; it's about Him, His Spirit, anointing and ability. The many thoughts calm down and my mind become rested and at peace. The more I dwell on Jesus, the more refreshed I become and new ideas started flowing. Therefore, continue coming to Jesus, keep basking in His love and presence. Become that well-watered garden: beautiful, flourishing, refreshing, and delightful.

Day 125—The Lord Is Your Strength

> The Lord God is my strength; He will make my feet like deer's feet, And He will make me walk on my high hills. (Habakkuk 3:19 NKJV)

As you do the ministry that God has for you, there can be times when you become weary and tired. Are you trying too hard by your own strength, tired and weary from so many challenges and problems? Come and rest in Jesus, for He is your strength. He strengthens you and takes you much further than you can go on your own.

He makes your feet like deer's feet. The deer has legs that leap and jump gracefully over mountains, streams, rivers, and other rough places. As the deer leaps over rough mountainsides, over thorny and stony ground, the thick hooves protect the deer from harm and injury. It is like a strong cushion that softens every leap and provides traction on soft, wet, and hard surfaces. Because of the hooves working with the strong legs, the deer is able to move gracefully, almost effortlessly regardless of how rough the terrain and at a top speed of thirty-five miles per hour.

As you come to Jesus, He strengthens you with His strength and gives you the ability to leap over challenges and trials, rough patches, and thorny problems that seem so insurmountable. He smoothens the path and makes your feet like deer feet so that you are able to move gracefully over all the obstacles and challenges that are in your way. It doesn't matter how high and challenging your mountains and hills are; walk and leap with confidence and strength.

We can choose to struggle on our own, or we can choose to come to Jesus, who has already suffered on our behalf. We can choose to be frustrated, weary, and worn out, or we can come to Jesus and receive His life. As we rest in Him, He lifts us up in His peace, joy and grace; empowering, strengthening and enabling us to overcome all trials and challenges.

Come to Jesus now. See His person; how lovely and wonderful He is. Enjoy and bask in His presence. Be comforted and be filled with His peace and rest.

Day 126—Be Renewed in Your Mind

> And do not be conformed to this world, but be transformed
> by the renewing of your mind, that you may prove what *is*
> that good and acceptable and perfect will of God. (Romans
> 12:2 NKJV)

In the world is strife, struggles, schemes, cunning, and stress. The world is consumed with greed, fear, worries, hopelessness, bondages, and addictions that destroy. As we walk in faith and in the calling of God, it is easy to lose sight and fall into the world's ways of strife and struggle to accomplish His work. God desires for us to continually renew our minds by His truth, by His grace, and by faith, so that we stay in His grace and not fall into the world's way.

George Mueller was a man of great faith who trusted God to take care of orphans in Bristol, England in the 1800s. He built several orphanages that were home to a few thousand orphans. He had many testimonies of God's provision and supply for the needs of the orphans. Most importantly was how he would start each morning in the Lord's presence, feeding on Him, seeing His love, and receiving from Him until he was happy and satisfied. Rested in the Lord, he was able to believe Him for all the needs of the orphans. And God was faithful. Food, money for clothes, education, and buildings were supernaturally provided!

Continue to renew your mind to God's love and truth. See God's provision and supply for you. See His peace and joy. Come to Him daily for provision and strength for all that He has called you to do.

When you do that, you stay in the perfect will of God, living and serving out of the fullness of His heavenly abundant provision for you. You rest in His wisdom, love, peace, ability, provision and refreshing. In that place, you are set free from fears, anxieties and weariness. And you serve out of the abundance that Jesus gives, filled with His love, peace and joy. You are truly His light to the world. Hallelujah!

Day 127—What Do You Let Your Thoughts Dwell On?

> Finally, brothers and sisters, whatever is true, whatever is noble, whatever is right, whatever is pure, whatever is lovely, whatever is admirable—if anything is excellent or praiseworthy—think about such things. (Philippians 4:8)

What do you allow to dwell in your thought life? Many thoughts come to us daily, triggered by people, the news, and what we read on social media. It does not matter how mature we are in the faith; the negative news and thoughts that we entertain can bring on fear, anxiety, regret, condemnation, anger, and bitterness.

As you grow in your walk, choose to dwell on what is true and of God: how much God loves us, and how He has already forgiven us through Jesus Christ, His Son, so that we now have a place in His love, peace, and joy where all things are possible because of Him.

Let your thoughts dwell on Christ, who is true, noble, right, pure, lovely, admirable, excellent, and totally praiseworthy. When we think on these things, we put on the mind of Christ. Praise the Lord that He has given us His mind so we can think like Him. Let your mind always think about such things as the glory of God and not the gory of man.

Do not let the problems and troubles at hand overwhelm you and cause you to lose sight of the wonderful love that God has for you and how precious you are to Him.

Instead, dwell on how marvellous it is that we have the Holy Spirit in us, and how He leads us and guides us. Rejoice because of His goodness and faithfulness. Only God alone is praiseworthy, excellent, trustworthy, and full of grace. When you dwell on these things, your spirit is strengthened, and you dwell in divine peace and security on unshakable ground.

Day 128—Let Your Words and Meditations Be Pleasing to God

> May the words of my mouth and the meditation of my heart
> be pleasing to you, O Lord, my Rock and my Redeemer.
> (Psalm 19:14 NLT)

If you have been meditating on and complaining about the symptoms coming against your body, your lack of finance, limited career opportunities, the way your relationships seem to fall apart, or the state of the world and getting fearful—stop. Renew your mind, your meditations, and the words of your mouth. Start meditating on Jesus and what He has done for you. Start declaring with your words who you are and what you have because of Him.

The words of our mouths and the meditation of our hearts that please God are those focussed on Jesus and His loveliness, beauty, majesty, love, grace, and compassion. Remember all that He has done for us at the cross, His resurrection, and His present-day ministry as our great High Priest seated at God's right hand, having defeated the enemy.

They are meditations on how wonderfully Jesus has restored us to righteousness, holiness, and perfection by His finished work at the cross. They are meditations on how loved, well supplied, and protected we are because of what Jesus has done for us. He alone deserves all praise and glory.

Let Jesus be the meditation of your heart. Let His love, grace, and truth be your meditation and the words that proceed from your mouth. Use your words to confess and declare His goodness and grace. These are the words and meditations that send a sweet aroma to our heavenly Father.

Not only does this please our Father, but as you do so, you shall rise above whatever that has come against you. Praising Him and meditating on Him opens for you the floodgate of joy, peace, love, provision, and blessings that He has already attained for you by His finished work at the cross.

Day 129—In Christ, You Are a King and a Priest

> To Him who loved us and washed us from our sins in His own blood, and made us kings and priests to God, to Him *be* glory and dominion forever and ever. Amen. (Revelation 1:5b–6 NKJV)

Jesus has made you a king. A king reigns and is not pushed around. A king has the highest place and authority. A king's word has weight and power. When he gives a word, an order, it will be done. Realise that this is how your Father sees you, as a king. He has placed you in a high and esteemed position and given you the authority that comes with it.

Don't allow the enemy or defeating thoughts to push you around or run you down. Start to see yourself as your Father sees you, a king in a high position of authority. Start to use your authority and words to put things in place. Start declaring what you want to see happen in your life and the lives of those you love.

Your Father sees you as a priest, someone who has the right to come before Him and make your petitions, as well as those of others, known to Him. As a priest, you represent not just yourself but those you love, those in your circle of influence, to God.

What a powerful combination that our heavenly Father has bestowed on you because of Jesus. You are a king and a priest. Therefore, start to speak as one and call forth what God has for you and your loved ones.

- I can do all things in Christ who strengthens me.
- I shall live and fulfil all the good plans and purposes that God has for me.
- No evil can overtake me, and I will dwell in the house of the Lord forever.
- My children will grow in favour with God and man and live out the full purposes that God has for them.
- They shall be protected from the world's thoughts and ways and will grow strong in His love and truth.

Day 130—Living the Victorious Life in Christ

> Be filled with the Spirit, speaking to one another in psalms
> and hymns and spiritual songs, singing and making melody
> in your heart to the Lord. (Ephesians 5:18b–19 NKJV)

A victorious life with Christ is one where when challenges and obstacles come against you, when fears and worries try to get you, they cannot crush or defeat you. You continue to live with hope, faith and joy, trusting that God will take you through. It's where lack, anger, destructive habits and behaviours take a back seat, and you continue in peace and love, thriving and fulfilling the desires that God has placed in you. You speak words that bring healing, comfort, and edification to others.

You ask, 'How do I live this life in the midst of so many challenges?' Today's scripture tells us to be filled with the Holy Spirit; to speak in psalms, hymns, and spiritual songs; and to make melody in our hearts to the Lord.

We could stay in our rational, emotional realm, endlessly chewing on and analysing the problems and challenges and getting into more fears and anxieties. Or we could spend time in God's Word, to graze and meditate on His goodness, love, and faithfulness. And praise Him with our words, with songs, with a hymn and allow His Spirit to dominate us with His peace and joy. When we come together, we could talk endlessly of the challenges we face, the issues in the world. Or we could pray and praise Him with a hymn, a psalm, a song, or words of worship, glorifying Him and strengthening our hearts with gladness.

Come and fill your heart with happy melodies to the Lord, and sing of His love and goodness. Put aside the worries and anxieties. Come praising Him and build your faith and trust to receive what He has for you. One day at a time, start to turn your eyes from problems and instead glorify Him with praises. Sing songs to Him in your heart and refuse to allow those fears and worries to hijack you. Do this day after day and start to grow stronger in His joy and peace, and begin to walk in the victory that He has for you.

Day 131—Pray and Praise!

> But at midnight Paul and Silas were praying and singing hymns to God…… Suddenly there was a great earthquake, so that the foundations of the prison were shaken; and immediately all the doors were opened and everyone's chains were loosed. (Acts 16:25–26, NKJV)

Paul and Silas were thrown in prison, but instead of grumbling or complaining about being in prison, feeling defeated, being fearful about what might happen to them, being despondent and angry, they spent their time praying and singing hymns. As they were praying and singing out loud, there was a great earthquake, the foundations of the prison were shaken, all the doors were opened, and everyone's chains came loose. They walked out of prison.

When we pray and praise the Lord, He is right there. In His presence, wonderful things happen. The supernatural, spiritual realm is stirred, bringing on God's solution for the challenges we are facing. Bondage is broken, God's provision and favour flow, healing happens, joy and peace replace fear and tension, rest replaces weariness, and hearts are softened. God's unlimited resources and restoration flow when we give praise and glory to God from the abundance of our hearts.

Do you complain about your problem or symptoms? Remember, you are a child of God and His resources are available for you. These problems and challenges cannot defeat you unless you let them.

Come to the Lord. Lift your eyes to Jesus. Make it a lifestyle to pray and praise Him at all times. It positions you to rest in Jesus and receive all the solutions that God has for you. That is the secret to why some are so blessed, tasting the goodness of God and always in peace and joy regardless of the situation.

Whatever you are facing, take time now and praise Jesus for His love, mercy and grace. Think of the blessings that you have received and thank Him. Day after day, practice praise and thanksgiving and see your life lifted.

Day 132—Encourage and Build Up Each Other

[Christ] died for us, that whether we wake or sleep, we should live together with Him. Therefore comfort each other and edify one another, just as you also are doing. (1 Thessalonians 5:9–11 NKJV)

When New Covenant believers come together, it is unlike the gatherings of the world, where people are sizing one another up according to what they wear, where they live, what they drive, and where gossip abounds.

Instead, Jesus ought to be the centre of our fellowship, where we speak words of blessings, encouragement, edification and comfort to build each other to the fullness of Christ. Believers point each other to Christ, reminding each other of their identity in Christ, of their son-ship, and of the authority that Jesus has given to each one.

We share our challenges so that others can pray in agreement to see the manifestation of God's love and might. When New Covenant believers come together, it is a most blessed time where Jesus is magnified, and His presence becomes so strong that all can receive from Him peace, love, joy, healing, restoration, and solutions to challenges. All are strengthened in His presence and are able to give to one another so that we leave filled with His peace and loveliness, strengthened to face the next day.

We live in a fallen world where trials and challenges still abound. We are bombarded with values contrary to God's. Obstacles abound to keep us from doing the things that the Holy Spirit has put in our hearts to do to bless others. We all need encouragement and edification from one another to stay on course.

If we labour in anything, let us labour to become New Covenant believers who are full of Christ, who are led by the Holy Spirit, and who seek to speak comfort, edification, and encouragement to one another!

Day 133—Give Thanks in Everything

> In everything give thanks; for this is the will of God in
> Christ Jesus for you. (1 Thessalonians 5:18 NKJV)

Today's scripture tells us that because we belong to Jesus, God's will for us is that we give thanks in everything. It is not because God needs our thanksgiving or gratitude. When we give thanks, it lifts us to walk more victoriously in His provision, peace, joy, and blessings.

An attitude of giving thanks keeps us from looking at ourselves and what we think we are short of. It keeps us from being bitter and steeped in self-pity. It also keeps us from becoming prideful, thinking we are so good. When we look for all the little blessings in our lives and give thanks for them, instead of grumbling about what we don't have or getting frenzied and worried, our spirits are lifted and our joy is restored.

When we give thanks, we humble ourselves and acknowledge that we did not bring any good thing upon ourselves. Instead, we acknowledge God's goodness, kindness, faithfulness, and love for us. When we humble ourselves and become more Jesus-focussed, we position ourselves to receive so much more fully from Him.

Christ has given us every wonderful blessing, provision, protection, joy, and peace so we can live victoriously for His glory. The key to walking in the fullness and abundance He has for you is to always pray without ceasing, praise Him, give thanks in everything, and dwell in the peace and joy that Jesus has for you.

Will you praise Jesus and give thanks to Him for everything He has done for you? Will you think of the things for which you can thank Him and speak out and thank Him out loud? Will you do that every day, every hour, and all the time? If you make this a daily practice, He will fill your heart with such a peace and joy and victory over all challenges.

Day 134—Always Be Joyful

Always be joyful. Never stop praying. (1 Thessalonians
5:16–17 NLT)

Today's scripture tells us to always be joyful. You may ask how that is possible.
The demands are so great, the challenges and expectations are overwhelming,
the bills are piling, the creditors are calling, and you see no solution in sight.

But your joy is not based on what you see or don't see, or what you feel. You
can be joyful because the Holy Spirit, who is the Spirit of joy, now resides in
you. Through Him you have already been given God's joy. Joy is the culture
of heaven, one of the fruits of the Spirit, and because the Spirit resides in you,
this fruit is yours to partake of. You can exercise it regardless of the external
circumstances or your feelings.

The key to be joyful is to fix your eyes on Jesus, who He is, His majesty and
glory, see all His wonderful works, see that He has already given you the Holy
Spirit who is love, peace and joy. Staying in Christ and staying joyful, you
take a heavenly posture in the face of natural challenges. It strengthens you
against the enemy and what the world tries to throw at you.

We are exhorted to never stop praying. Praying is simply talking to God,
thanking Him, calling forth in agreement with God's Word the good plans
that He has already ordained for your life, praising Him, and giving Him
honour and glory. Praying is also listening and hearing Him as He shares with
you His plans and desires, giving you directions and council, downloading
ideas and thoughts, showing you open doors, and speaking His love, peace,
and joy to you. Praying is humbling ourselves and acknowledging that we are
dependent on God. Nothing is too small or insignificant for Him.

No matter the circumstances, stay joyful and pray with thanksgiving! Take
time now and invite the Lord to sit with you. Quieten your thoughts. Take
time and allow His peace to flood your heart and mind with His joy. Bask in
that peace and be filled with His love and joy.

Day 135—See Trials as a Way to Grow

> My brethren, count it all joy when you fall into various trials
> knowing that the testing of your faith produces patience. But
> let patience have its perfect work, that you may be perfect
> and complete, lacking nothing. (James 1:2–4 NKJV)

The victory that we have in Christ does not mean that the life of a believer is a problem-free bed of roses. It's not a life of happy partying to show how blessed we are. In the same vein, some think this victorious life means having no problems or challenges. So when these come along, they are too ashamed to share and have people pray with them. They see problems as a sign of failure, a sign that they are not blessed. Do you or someone you know think this way?

God does not send trials and problems. They are a natural part of this fallen world that we live in. There is no condemnation when trials come along. At the same time, they also cannot overwhelm you because Christ has given you the victory over them. Today's scripture tells us to be glad when trials come.

You ask, 'How do I find joy in trials? What can they do for me?' They are opportunities for you to grow in faith and trust in Jesus. He longs for you to know that He has you in His hands and that all will be well. When you come to Him, His Spirit strengthens you and lifts you to a place of rest, peace, joy, and hope. He gives you His wisdom to know what to do, and how to move. He is able to work things out for you.

As you abide in Him, you calm down, putting aside your fears and letting His patience, peace and love form in you. You become more complete in Christ, having His patience to endure.

God loves you and desires above all to see you come to maturity in Christ. The ultimate goal of a believer is not just about living a blessed life. It is about being blessed and then being transformed to be more Christ-like and have His patience, compassion, love, kindness, and goodness. It is about being set apart for God's purpose as the Body of Christ here on earth, blessing others. That is the true joy of a believer!

Day 136—Rejoice in Suffering

> Not only that, but we rejoice in our sufferings, knowing that suffering produces endurance, and endurance produces character, and character produces hope. (Romans 5:3–4 ESV)

Trials can easily come upon a believer especially when you hold values contrary to those of the world. Believers are persecuted just for following Jesus. The reason that the world hates Jesus is because the unrepentant world is still under the dominion of Satan. Those who refuse Christ are still under Satan's dominion. And he is able to wield his influence over them. Just as he can also wield his influence over the natural world.

But as a child of God, you have no fear. In Christ you are protected. You already have an eternal home in love, peace, joy, in eternal fellowship with our wonderful heavenly Father. That is why the enemy is so upset! He cannot touch you or harm you at all. He can try to influence people to come against you, or circumstances to work against you but in Christ you will remain unharmed.

Today's scripture tells us to rejoice when sufferings come. It could be suffering because of believing Christ, having different values from the world or simply suffering the effects of this life. Jesus Himself set us an example. He came and suffered and right to the end, He was kind and forgiving to those who tortured Him: 'Father, forgive them for they know not what they do.' Finally, He brought us the life of God and the gift of His Spirit.

When trials come, rejoice and look to Jesus, meditate on His Word, marvel at His loveliness, abide in Him, thank Him for what He has done for you. Rejoice for the wonderful salvation He has given you. As you rejoice and abide in Him, His presence with you establishes you in joy, peace, in patient love, endurance and hope. You become an overcomer! Continue to abide in Him, and become a fitting body of Christ here on earth, able to go out and share His love and truths with the world. Amen.

Day 137—We May Be Perplexed but Never in Despair

> We are hard-pressed on every side, yet not crushed; we are perplexed, but not in despair; persecuted, but not forsaken; struck down, but not destroyed. (2 Corinthians 4:8–9 NJKV)

We will have trials as long as we are in this world. It doesn't matter what your calling is or that you are serving the Lord. The trials respect no one. When trials come to us; when disaster strikes, or illness and disease present itself; when false accusations are heaped on you, or the bills piled high; or when you lose your position, know that Christ is there. He is your strength and the one who lifts you.

In Christ, you have a real and present help. His Spirit lives in you, enabling you, enlightening you, empowering you, and keeping you in His joy and peace. He loves you, He lives in you, and He will always sustain you.

Our hope in life is not for everything to always work out fine or for everything to always go our way. Our hope is in Jesus, who keeps us from being crushed, who will never forsake us, who will never leave us alone without help, and who will always restore us. In Christ, despite disasters and trials, we can say all is well because in Christ, we may face trials and problems, but they will not crush us.

We may be perplexed, but He will not leave us in despair. We may be persecuted, but He will not forsake us. No matter what the enemy throws at us, he cannot destroy us. Therefore, beloved, be encouraged. Things may seem hopeless, and you may feel helpless and fearful. Do not despair, and do not go by your feelings. The fact is that Jesus is totally with you, shielding you, helping you, and loving you. The Spirit of God in you will uphold you. He will not allow you to be crushed and destroyed.

Jesus is truly your strength, and the power of the Holy Spirit is there to bring you the final victory in His perfect peace and joy!

Day 138—Suffer for the Right Reason!

> But let none of you suffer as a murderer, a thief, an evildoer,
> or as a busybody in other people's matters. (1 Peter 4:15)

Sometimes we bring sufferings upon ourselves because of our wrongdoings, greed, selfishness and unloving actions. This scripture tells us not to suffer as a murderer, thief, evildoer or busybody. A believer who suffered because he stole, cheated and lied or who out of greed, invested unwisely, needs to repent (realise he need not resort to the world's ways). What he suffered was merely the consequences of his wrongdoings! Yet when he repents, God, in His love and mercy, will surely embrace Him and even restore his losses. And in turning over a new leaf, he can be a testimony of the grace and goodness of God.

The suffering that is worthy of Christ is suffering for His name's sake: enduring persecution because of your beliefs and values in Him. You endure insults because you stay faithful and continue speaking His truth and love. You suffer a loss in income and separation from family and friends because you responded to that abundance in your heart to go and share His love to the nations. You chose to love unlovable people, enduring heartaches and pain, because you see their potential in Christ. You are wrongly accused and slandered and instead of retaliating and fighting back, you draw closer to Christ, seeing that He went through much worse for you at the cross.

Through no fault of yours, you were caught in a calamity or an accident, or hit with an illness. You suffered a financial loss, you suffered because of the mistakes of loved ones. You did your best, but your child is wayward and rebellious. Instead of becoming bitter and overwhelmed by fears and anxieties, you allow Christ to keep you in His peace and rest through the trial.

In the face of suffering, pray and ask the Lord for His constant help to keep you anchored to Him as your hope and joy. When you do that, suffering cannot defeat you. Enduring righteous sufferings, anchored in Christ as your hope and joy, you shine His light in a troubled world, drawing people to Him. What joy to be able to shine Christ for others!

Day 139—In Christ, You Dwell in the City of the Living God

> But you have come to Mount Zion and to the city of the living God, the heavenly Jerusalem, to an innumerable company of angels. (Hebrews 12:22 NJKV)

Mount Sinai was where the Law was given to Moses. Mount Sinai represented a place of bondage to works and self-effort, working to keep the demands and requirement of the Law to please God.

Mount Zion, on the other hand, represents the city of the living God, where He freely welcomes us to fellowship with Him. By Jesus's finished work, we have been forgiven; we have been made holy and now dwell in Mount Zion, where we can fellowship freely with God.

Dear friend, in Christ you have come to the immense blessings of being in relationship with your heavenly Father; you are forgiven, loved, and accepted. You have come to the freedom in the Spirit that has been freely poured out on you. You have His life, His anointing, and His essence. What moves Him moves you, and you have a divine identity.

No more striving and driving by your own efforts and smarts. Yield to His power, compassion, love, and ability; then you can overcome all things. You have come to the abundance of life that our heavenly Father has for you, and you've been filled with divine purpose. You're living in this fallen world, but our eternal reality is heaven, with all its wonders and glory. We have been made children of God, and we have access to the resources of the heavenly realm to live victoriously, overcoming all the circumstances of this fallen world.

God loves you and wants you set free from a spirit of bondage to your own effort, work, fear, lack, and striving. He wants you to walk freely in His love, provision, abilities, and the works He has for you. Come to Christ at all times, look to Him, and rest in Him, because in Him dwells your freedom, peace, joy, purpose, and destiny.

Day 140—He Will Not Leave You nor Forsake You

> For He Himself has said, 'I will never leave you nor forsake you.' (Hebrews 13:5b NKJV)

God showed His love for the children of Israel by moving with them wherever they went—as a pillar of cloud in the day, keeping them cool, and as a pillar of fire at night, keeping them warm. Today, Jesus has completed the work of redemption, and His Spirit lives in you and me. This is God's commitment to us to be our guiding light, the source of power, strength, comfort, protection, and companionship for us from His Spirit that lives within us.

How awesome that our God is present with us at all times, good or bad! His joy, peace, companionship, wisdom, counsel, and protection is always there. He also longs for our companionship and fellowship. But in the busyness of our lives, it is easy to forget that He is right there within us. When we are caught up in the trials and challenges, it's easy to forget that He is right there and that His resources and solutions are available to us, if only we turn to Him.

Come to Him often. At all times, delight in His companionship and draw from Him and His endless supply of strength, joy, peace, wisdom, and love. Especially when you are facing hardship, know that He is right there with you. He will never leave you or forsake you. When you are sick, down, discouraged, overwhelmed, beset with relationship problems, persecuted, or feeling all alone, He is right there with you.

He loves you, He delights in you, He takes great pleasure in you, and He desires to see you walk in righteousness and wholeness. But above all, He desires that you walk in fellowship and companionship with Him.

He beckons you to come to Him at all times. As you continue to abide in Him, your path will shine brighter and brighter and you will grow from glory to glory! Amen.

Salvation Prayer

If you would like Jesus to be the Lord and Master of your life, or if you are not sure whether He is your Lord and Master, pray this prayer from your heart and let His peace and joy fill you.

> Lord Jesus, I invite You to be the Lord and Master of my life. Thank You for dying on the cross for me, forgiving all my sins, and giving me Your righteousness. I thank You for Your peace and joy that now reside in me. Help me as I learn to grow in greater understanding of who You are and all that You have done for me. Help me submit all my ways and thoughts to You. In Jesus's name, I pray. Amen.

Thank you for taking the time to read this devotional. Please feel free to write to me if you have any questions. If you have been touched, affected, or impacted in any way by this book, I'd love to hear from you.

Email me at helenteoct@gmail.com.